To the Reader

As the stock market crashed in America and triggered the Great Depression, and Europe was on the road to World War II, William Gray was worrying about finding a better way to help children learn to read. Gray, one of the nation's leading reading experts, believed children would read more easily if their schoolbooks included illustrations that *showed* a child's world—a colorful world full of fun, suspense and surprise — rather than just *describing* one. When words were used, he knew they would have to ring true.

So beginning in the late 1920s, Gray began to build the world of Dick and Jane, featuring characters created by a reading consultant named Zerna Sharp, for the educational publisher Scott, Foresman and Company. What Gray and Sharp and teams of passionate educators, writers, illustrators and editors produced was the map for the classic illustrated book series that taught eighty-five million children how to read from the 1930s through the 1960s.

Growing Up with Dick and Jane takes us back to the seductive watercolor world where we learned how to read. It's a world where night never comes, knees never scrape, parents never yell and the fun never stops. For schoolchildren who lived through the Depression and World War II, the world of Dick and Jane must have read like a dream. But for baby boomers lucky enough to escape the suffering of their parents and to be born into a postwar paradise, the stories they read in the first months of the first grade felt like their everyday suburban lives.

Growing Up with Dick and Jane steps back in time and reenters the world of mid-century childhood. Remember holding a Dick and Jane primer for the first time? Remember the thrill—the exact moment—when you *knew* you could read? Here it is again, the green grass and the blue skies. And here are Dick and Jane and Sally, Mother and Father and Spot— the happy, happy family. Now, as grown-ups, we can see a bigger picture—how the optimism in these little books, seen alongside the turbulent events of the times, together tell the story of a country defining, pursuing and living the American Dream.

Growing Up with

Dick and Jane

Learning and Living
the American Dream

by CAROLE KISMARIC *and* MARVIN HEIFERMAN
Preface by Bob Keeshan, creator of Captain Kangaroo

A Lookout Book

CollinsPublishers
A Division of HarperCollinsPublishers

Contents

Preface 7

Dreaming the American Dream 8

Living the American Dream 54

Growing Up with Dick and Jane 90

The World of Dick and Jane
Bob Keeshan, creator of Captain Kangaroo

I grew up with Dick and Jane, was a contemporary of theirs. You see, I was born, as were Dick and Jane, in the year 1927. Perhaps we even share a birthday.

The world that William Gray and Zerna Sharp created for Dick and Jane was my world. They seemed to suffer little during America's Great Depression. I didn't even *know* there was a depression until I entered my sophisticated teens and became more aware of the world and reality. It wasn't that my father was wealthy; he was not, but we were fortunate to have him well placed in the grocery business, and that insulated our family from much of the hurt that was being endured by others.

I lived in what would now be called suburbia, though we didn't know that at the time. I had nice friends, a nice home, wonderful parents, a couple of dogs but no cats. The ice cream vendor drove by each warm summer evening, bell tinkling, neighborhood children screaming in delight. I sat with many of the other kids on the grassy slopes alongside our homes and played exciting games of imagination. We frightened each other with thrilling ghost stories. Yes, we did believe in ghosts. What would the world be without such tantalizing thoughts?

It was, for me, the world of Dick and Jane, the world that *every* child should inhabit, a world with yellow brick roads, the security of parental love, full stomachs and overflowing hearts filled with warm feelings. Such a world was also filled with the awesome discoveries of childhood, each as tasty as that summer evening's ice cream bar. For most children living in the thirties, Dick and Jane could only be a wonderful dream, a dream of what might be. I was fortunate enough to live the dream.

My world changed in the forties, just as Dick and Jane's did in the fifties and sixties. There were no people quite like Dick and Jane in the Marine Corps, and I was forever transformed. I was "growing up," and World War II accelerated that process. Then along came my children, the baby boomers, and their life was often closer to the ideal. But their world was changing, too, particularly the world of nurturing. The "nurturing place," the family, was being restructured. Mom and Dad sometimes decided they would be better off apart; Mom went to work outside the home, and single-parent families became commonplace.

Highways and jet planes made us a mobile society, and the extended family of grandparents, uncles, aunts and cousins was often miles away when we needed them to help raise the kids. Today's is a very different world from the world of Dick and Jane. Along with the strain placed on the family, much good has come of change. We have become more honest in recognizing that we are not a cookie cutter society. We are far from perfect, but at least we're more realistic and a lot more honest. We are pluralistic, and in that pluralism resides our strength. Most of us have tried to raise our children to understand that American ideal.

By the time *Captain Kangaroo* went on the air in 1955, I had already spent eight years developing programs for children. Television programs such as my first, *Howdy Doody,* were considered by many in the educational community as a threat to good reading habits in children. By 1955, I felt quite to the contrary. I knew that constructive programming could inform children and encourage them to seek more knowledge of a subject that they first learned about on television. The worst fears of educators and reading experts were unfounded. Children read more than ever today. In over nine thousand *Captain Kangaroo* programs we read thousands of books, some of them again and again. We modeled reading habits for children, and today's adults—yesterday's children—often relate how those reading habits became, for them, a lifelong pleasure.

Foster imagination, provide security, feed the mind of the child as well as the body, show your love as well as declaring it, and you will be building self-confidence. Be patient, allow a child to learn from mistakes. "You can do it" should be the most often repeated words of love from parent to child. A child entering kindergarten who has been shown that he or she is capable of accomplishment and high self-esteem is a winner.

Childhood, for every child, should be as close as possible to the ideal world of Dick and Jane. Sometimes the ugliness of our surroundings gets in the way. Never let that ugliness come from you, the parent. With love and security—and an occasional ice cream bar—our children will turn out like Dick and Jane. I'll let you in on a secret. The Dicks and Janes of this world grow into happy human beings. Love!

1. Dreaming the

American Dream

The Declaration of Independence doesn't guarantee that childhood will be a carefree, happy time. In fact, the notion of childhood as a time of innocence, illustrated so convincingly in the Dick and Jane books, was a new idea just beginning to take hold in the 1930s. When the youngest Pilgrims touched down on Plymouth Rock, they had to work hard to survive, helping their mothers and fathers in any way they could. Life was tough in the New World, and it stayed tough. For two hundred years, most Americans eked out their livings on farms, and even the youngest children made a difference hauling water and tools, feeding animals, minding younger siblings, doing chores around the homestead.

In the mid-nineteenth century, when farm families and new immigrants began settling in cities in search of economic opportunity, their working children made another kind of difference, by adding their twenty-five cents a day to the family's pot. And by the century's end, America was experiencing an enormous economic expansion as the industrial revolution created millions of jobs. Many working-class and immigrant children, laboring fourteen-hour days in stifling mills, mines or factories, were valuable assets to bosses, because their nimble little fingers could often outperform those of any adult. Children who didn't have to work were expected to be self-reliant too, even if they spent their day in school instead of at a factory. Discipline was the order of the day. At home, around the dinner table, on the streets, in shops and in churches, children were to be clean and well-behaved, seen but not heard.

Whether children worked in the mines, fields or sweatshops, or folded their hands neatly on their school desks, the very nature of childhood continued to be contested. Philosophers, educators and labor reformers championed the idea of childhood as a sacred time. Child labor laws, protecting children from on-the-job abuse, boosted the notion of youth as a sentimental safe harbor. By the end of the nineteenth century, the majority of states had passed laws making elementary school attendance compulsory.

At the same time, society was starting to pay attention to children in new and different ways. Sigmund Freud was one of the first to argue that children were instinctual creatures, with sexual and psychological needs. Psychologist G. Stanley Hall, who headed the Child Study movement,

1930

During the Depression children saw family shops boarded up or family farms taken over by banks. While fathers traveled to find work or sold apples on street corners and mothers scrimped and saved, crafty youngsters raised money any way they could to contribute to the family or—with a nickel saved—to go to the movies.

Nothing would be too good

endorsed children's needs to express themselves freely, to act and speak like children, to be free of constraining adult morality. By the late nineteenth century, philosopher and educator John Dewey challenged old-fashioned models of education based on rote learning and administered by authoritarian teachers, whose job was to bend a child's will. Dewey's vision respected children as individuals whose intelligence should be stimulated and whose imagination could be encouraged to flourish.

A progressive vision of childhood was taking hold by the early twentieth century. New textbooks, filled with colorful pictures and lively verses, reflected this idealized world of children. Cheaper paper and high-volume printing techniques made it possible for each child to have his or her own reader. Progressive educators began to operate on the premise that each child was an individual who learned differently.

Changes in elementary education paralleled changes in American society. The idea of childhood as a wonderful, unique stage in life so charmed the culture that childhood became a special time to be cherished and protected. Of course, hard work and good deeds were not forgotten. Children were still expected to behave properly and help out. But there was a sense, at the start of the new century, that childhood was something of a dreamworld.

This dream for children, and the larger American Dream, the firm belief that hard work leads to prosperity, turned into a nightmare when the stock market crashed in 1929. It took two years of further declines in stock prices and in the volume of business for the Great Depression to hit Americans with its full force. In the bust of the thirties, with cash scarce and corporate profits collapsed, salaries were cut. A record high of 25 percent of the work force was unemployed. It felt like a vicious, unending cycle. People lost faith in a government that aided banks and big business but did little to help them. Confidence shaken and marked for life with the guilt of personal failure, adults and children alike bartered, begged and stole to survive, or they went hungry. Feeling betrayed and defeated, men and women put aside their dreams of happy families and a future.

Shirley Temple's curly locks won the hearts of Americans dispirited by the Great Depression. By 1938, the ten-year-old had starred in over a dozen movies, such as *Little Miss Marker* (1934) and *Poor Little Rich Girl* (1936) and earned top dollar at the box office.

This poster was distributed to 1,400 police chiefs, seeking information about the baby of aviation hero Charles A. Lindbergh, who was kidnapped from his crib on March 1, 1932. Outrage over the incident forced passage of the death penalty in federal kidnapping cases.

for children shielded from the Depression and

Maintaining the sanctity of childhood was nearly impossible. Parents couldn't indulge their children or shield them from hardship. Kids needed to help make ends meet. So by selling homegrown produce or scrounging through garbage cans for scraps, from trapping crabs and rabbits, kids brought money home. And whether they lived in the city or on the farm, they were expected to find ways of contributing.

For most middle-class kids, childhood was carefree only when they could escape from everyday life. Radio was free, and after school and every night families tuned in, staring at the dial until their imaginations let them wander along trails with the Lone Ranger, sneak down abandoned silver mines with Jack Armstrong—the all-American boy—or round up arch criminals at the Shadow's side. On Saturday afternoons, kids paid a nickel to enter a world of moody lighting, red carpets and velvet drapes. They stayed all day, watching Movietone newsreels, coming attractions, cliff-hanging serials, cartoons and then a double bill—a western and a musical featuring one of the many child stars of the era.

During the Depression, children became symbols of hope, of better things to come. The Dionne Quintuplets became an international sensation at their birth in 1934, as well-wishers cheered for the survival of five frail baby girls. In their darkest hours, Americans became obsessed with sunny Shirley Temple and her fifty-six curls. She and other glamorized child stars like Mickey Rooney, Judy Garland and Jackie Coogan lightened people's hearts as they sang and danced their way through the Depression. These pint-size movie stars projected all the characteristics of the ideal childhood that educators and reformers had been touting for decades.

As Americans wobbled back to economic stability, Hitler was marching on Poland, and Mussolini was goose-stepping through Rome. When parents pushed children through the turnstiles of New York's 1939 World's Fair, they were in no mood to sacrifice for the people whose lives were being devastated "over there" across the Atlantic. It took the shock of the Japanese bombing of Pearl Harbor to jolt the United States into battle. The war jump-started the American economy, as a massive defense effort created seventeen million new jobs. American men, women and chil-

The B-29 bomber was the ultimate air weapon of WWII. Its use against Japan was a turning point in the Pacific war, and it was used to drop the first atomic bomb on Hiroshima.

During WWII, advertisers, with few consumer goods to sell, focused on getting Americans to support the war. This 1944 Goodyear Tire Company ad shows that home front Americans could help the war effort by investing in U.S. Treasury Bonds.

WWII. Postwar affluence would assure kids the

dren vowed to work together to destroy the enemy they all agreed on, the totalitarian evil that threatened democracy and the American way of life.

If the Depression didn't defeat America, neither would fascism, whose threatening voices and faces kids learned to recognize from radio broadcasts, weekly newsreels, movie magazines, advertisements and posters that filled their schoolrooms and community centers. Kids were trained to identify enemy planes, played war games in which they raged against Nazis and the Japanese, collected tin foil from gum and cigarette packs for recycling, gathered milkweed pods for stuffing life preservers, planted Victory gardens to supply their own food, and even turned in their toys as scrap materials.

The terrible war did wonderful things for the American economy. Factories that made lipstick made bullet cases. Assembly lines that produced cars churned out tanks. Money was everywhere. In the first six months of 1942, the government ordered $100 billion in defense equipment. Bank deposits reached record highs as personal savings jumped from $6.3 billion in 1940 to over $37 billion by

1945. Because of war shortages, people on the home front spent their money on the smaller pleasures of life. Movie box office receipts doubled from 1940 to 1945. Sales of cosmetics, self-help paperbacks, and musical instruments skyrocketed. Nightclubs, bars, hotels and resorts were jammed. Kids amused themselves with radio serials, cartoons and comic books. They listened to Kate Smith singing "When the Moon Comes Over the Mountain" and Bing Crosby promising a "White Christmas," and they put their faith in Superman.

With their eyes on victory, Americans' personal lives were in flux. Over thirty million people, a fifth of the population, moved from one part of the country to another, following soldiers and jobs. Doubling up, they lived with relatives in garages and stores and shared homes with strangers, believing that once the war was won, things would get better. Advertising, with few consumer goods to sell, promoted sacrifice as the path to future gain.

And though it brought wealth, the war had real costs: 407,316 Americans were killed, 670,846 came home wounded and 183,000 children were left fatherless. After

1940

Kids played war games and collected newspapers, tin foil and cans for scrap. Once a week, they used their dimes and quarters to buy War Bond Stamps, which they pasted in their books. The book held $18.75 worth of stamps, which could be exchanged for a $25 War Bond, redeemable in ten years.

As oily black smoke from Japanese bombs swirled over Pearl Harbor, the stunning news of the December 7, 1941, sneak attack reached Americans via radio. When President Roosevelt announced that America was at war, everyone was ready to join up; all told, nearly sixteen million Americans served in WWII.

best of everything. Americans were ready to

years of separation, families unraveled. Children had forgotten their fathers; returning servicemen didn't recognize their own children. The divorce rate had doubled. Men who experienced the trauma of war came home shattered, to reenter a world that wouldn't stop for them.

But soon enough, the lure of the future overtook the grim past. Even before the war ended, government and big business had been planning how to turn the booming wartime economy into a prosperous peacetime economy. The money, production lines, new materials and ingenuity that won the war could be directed toward the home front market. Americans were eager for upward mobility and to indulge the pleasures they had deferred during the war.

Americans were ready to move to Easy Street, but first they needed places to live. A returning GI could buy his own dream house on a little plot of land away from the busy cities, where his wife and kids could take a giant step up the ladder of opportunity. With $400 billion in government credit and guaranteed loans, home ownership grew 50 percent from 1940 to 1950. It was in this new suburbia,

a "Babyville" created to cater to children, that childhood finally became the paradise the government and advertisers had promised.

The postwar baby boom supplied America with a new generation of consumers to fulfill the expectations not only of parents, but also of economists who recognized the unprecedented scale of the market. Nothing would be too good for these tots who had been shielded from the impact of both the Depression and the war. Their parents, who ate beans during the Depression and Spam during the war, would soon be grilling steaks in their own backyards. Postwar affluence—and a belief in the permanence of upward mobility—would assure their children the best of everything. More attention, more toys, more security. In their Dick and Jane years, the phenomenal luck of this generation would become clear. Just like Dick and Jane in the stories they would read in first grade, these kids knew they were going to be special.

move to Easy Street, where childhood would

Of the thirteen million homes built in the decade after WWII, eleven million of them were in new suburban developments. The rapid sprawl of suburbia coincided with other major changes: new affluence and social mobility, rising marriage and birth rates, the ethic of family "togetherness."

be the promised paradise.

Dick

Dick is an all-American boy. Master of a little world that stretches from his screen door, across the green lawn, to a white picket fence. It's a world where winter never comes, and the neighbors are nowhere to be seen. It's a world in which troubles from the big world don't trickle down. No Depression. No World War. Surrounded by white space and innocence, Dick (never Richard) is a confident little guy. Dick looks sharp in his shorts and snappy striped polo shirts. When Dick says, "Look, look. Look up. Look up, up, up," everyone else on the page does. He speaks simply, directly, and gets what he wants. Why not?

He's the oldest of three adorable children and the most responsible. He watches out for his younger sisters. He works around the house. Dick waters the lawn, helps set the table and knows how to dial the telephone. He is a little man. Maybe that's why Mother and Father leave Dick alone.

Dick gets top billing in America's best-selling Dick and Jane readers because he is the best a boy can be. A role model for generations of boys, his storybook life is one fun-filled adventure after another, where problems get solved before big tears get shed. Dick is a real boy: always in motion. He climbs trees, rides a bike, flies a kite, and throughout his forty-year career, plays baseball, basketball and football. And Dick has Spot, the cocker spaniel he trains, feeds, walks, plays with and loves.

Dick is organized. He likes routines, because they make his life run smoothly. When his little world spins out of control, it's Dick who stops the runaway red wagon. It's Dick who finds a missing toy, a missing pet, a missing sister. It's Dick, not Father, who keeps order and resolves problems. And it's Dick who makes sure every story ends with a giggle or a smile. That's why we like Dick.

Dick is better than average. He's never, ever afraid, not like other six-year-olds, who sometimes have fears and bad dreams. Dick works and plays well with his sisters and friends and respects his parents and grandparents. He's not boisterous, competitive or mean. He never bullies, never punches, never kicks.

Never cries.

In fact, Dick never gets in trouble.

Little boys once behaved a lot like Dick. They shook hands with adults, never spoke out of turn, and did chores without expecting an allowance. During the Depression, Dick's charmed life was a daydream for boys who sold rags and bottles to bring home extra pennies for food. And during World War II, boys scanned the skies for enemy planes, wondering if they'd ever see their fathers again. Kids had no choice; they had to grow up fast and join America's fight against evil. Even fun had its edge. Games were war games. On Saturday afternoons, war movies

Talking Pictures
Dick and Jane's speech isn't as colorful as the illustrations that capture their true personalities. Dick's repertoire of expressions and gestures reveal his exemplary character traits: his attentiveness (he points things out because his vocabulary is limited); his joie de vivre (Dick often spreads his fingers, palms up, in delight or surprise); and his self-assurance and determination (hands on hips, feet spread) to be a little man.

were preceded by newsreels that showed real people, even children, dying.

It wasn't until after the war that Dick's trouble-free world and the world of real little boys seemed to become a mirror image of each other. If Dick never suffered, neither did the suburban kids of the 1950s, who were the center of their parents' world,

lucky to be born into a society exploding with toys, cars, breakfast cereals and multicolored appliances. Boys who read stories about Dick in school were also watching other little boys like Dick star on television shows. Living in a postwar paradise, they grew up believing that they were characters too, living out their lives in front of an adoring audience.

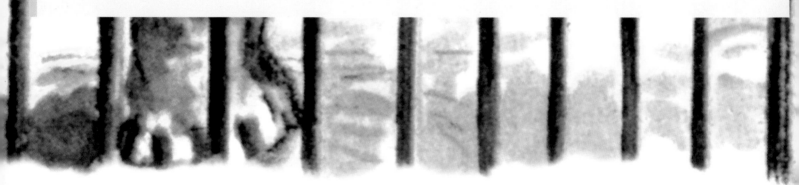

Good Boys, Bad Boys

The 1950s presented a multiple choice of boy wonders, Dick's peers, who either toed the line or broke the rules. Because many of them were entertainers seen week after week on TV, their behavior had to be a little less predictable than Dick's, to keep an audience from changing channels.

Timmy, the adopted orphan caretaker of *Lassie* (1954-74), first played by Tommy Rettig, was too good to be true. Unlike Dick, he was upstaged by his quicker-witted dog. Well-intentioned Beaver Cleaver, played by Jerry Mathers

on *Leave It to Beaver* (1957-63), might act selfishly but always knew when he had stepped over the line. A magnet for trouble, cute *Dennis the Menace*, a cartoon character turned TV star, played by Jay North (1959-63), was wild and almost too much for adults to handle.

Timmy Miller

Beaver Cleaver

Dennis the Menace

The Birth of Dick and Jane

Dick and Jane were born in 1927, when Zerna Sharp had an idea that would change how children learned to read. At the turn of the century, American textbooks were full of words. Excerpts from literature or Bible stories preached moralistic values, largely without the help of illustrations. By the 1920s, publisher Scott, Foresman and Company's Elson Readers, edited by reading authority William Gray, had reversed the equation. Big, colorful illustrations told their own stories, and the words with the pictures were simpler and fewer. A reading consultant for Scott Foresman, Sharp believed that children would read even better if they identified with the characters in the illustrations and read words that sounded familiar. She had been listening to kids carefully—how they used a limited vocabulary, spoke with uninhibited energy and repeated words for emphasis.

Sharp pitched her ideas to William Gray, who hired her to develop a family of characters that he could fold into his scientific approach to teaching reading. A revolutionary textbook concept was born. Sharp and a team of editors, consultants, writers, psychologists and illustrators sketched out the main characters and early story lines. After trial and error, they were given names, easy-to-remember four-letter words, Dick and Jane. No last name was necessary, for Dick and Jane were meant to represent Everyboy and Everygirl.

The editorial team that Sharp now supervised went on to create a curriculum of reading books that was interesting from a first-grader's point of view because they reflected a six-year-old's activities and language. The books were more "readable" than earlier textbooks and used attractive illustrations, large legible print and well-written stories full of humor, action, climaxes and suspense. The readers were simple enough for children to experience success reading them, and equally important, teachers would experience success in teaching them. The characters Dick and Jane first appeared in all the stories in the 1930 Elson Basic Reader pre-primer.

Zerna Sharp William S. Gray

The books were a huge success. Children loved what they saw in Eleanor Campbell's accurately researched, beautifully printed, colorful illustrations. They learned the words that went along with the pictures, using the "whole word" method that taught children to recognize complete words by sight, instead of phonetically sounding words out, letter by letter. Teachers encouraged their pupils to think about the characters' actions and thoughts, and to put themselves in Dick and Jane's place, deepening their connection to the characters and to reading.

The educational techniques and the "look" of the books had been a bold step in educational publishing, and they worked. By the 1950s, 80 percent of the first-graders in the United States who were learning to read were growing up with Dick and Jane.

Jane

Jane is a dream of a girl—pretty, bright and bright-eyed. Stable, responsible, Jane has Ginger Rogers's grace and June Allyson's wholesomeness. She's smart and down-to-earth. Yet for all her charms, Jane is second banana in a famous brother-sister act. She hovers on the outskirts of the action—always there if someone needs her—watching Dick hang confidently from a tree or Sally willfully tear down the street in her little metal pedal car. But Jane is not prissy. She might not skate as well as Dick, or run as fast, but it doesn't stop her from trying.

There's a lot to envy about Jane. Every time she walks onto the page, she's wearing something new. She gardens in a salmon pink dress, she paints in a flowered print dress, she rides a pony wearing a red dress and blue sweater, and she shops in a polka-dot dress. Jane looks like what every little girl dreams about. Her perky dresses never wrinkle or get dirty. She's so neat that even Spot and Puff know enough not to jump on her. Her blond, wavy hair is not too curly, like Shirley Temple's, not too frizzy, like Little Orphan Annie's. Jane's not too fat or too thin. Jane is a lucky girl, with nothing to cry or sulk about. Dick never teases her.

Sugar and Spice

Jane may have been too good to be true. That left the door open in popular culture for girls who didn't have brothers, docile personalities, ordinary pets or perfect manners. None of them had as many outfits, but they still captured the imagination of the American public.

Chunky, dark-haired Nancy (b. 1940) had dark moods and lived in a single-parent home. Her partner in adventure was not a well-behaved brother but Sluggo, a bald, pseudo-tough slum kid. Lucy van Pelt (b. 1950) was the pushy neurotic of the *Peanuts* troupe. She tormented her foil, the meek Charlie Brown, and was often overshadowed by Snoopy, the brilliant beagle. Patty McCormack played Rhoda, an eight-year-old liar, cheat, arsonist and murderer, in the 1956 movie *The Bad Seed*. Her evil behavior terrorized adults as well as good little children, on screen and in the audience.

Nancy

Rhoda Penmark

Lucy van Pelt

Mother and Father, Grandmother and Grandfather give her presents. Baby sister Sally adores her. Jane is cherished.

Jane doesn't make mistakes. She thinks before she speaks. She's thoughtful to her family and friends and is always willing to share what she has, especially her toys. Jane wants people to be happy. Even if she's perfectly capable of going off on her own—and occasionally does—Jane prefers to be one of the group, a part of the family, a link in her circle of friends. That's where she shines and shows how helpful, generous and fair a five-year-old can be.

More like a grown-up than a kid, Jane is a model girl for her time. She is modest, poised, unflappable. Jane watches everyone and everything carefully. She's learning how to set the table, bring in the laundry, go to the store, bake cakes and cookies. Jane thrives as a perfect younger sister, never upstaging Dick. She is a perfect older sister too, watching out for silly Baby Sally. Jane would rather work, helping Mother wash the floor, than run around the backyard. Home is the center of

Reading, the Old Way

Before Dick and Jane books were passed down the aisles in schools across the country in 1930, learning to read was a lot less fun. Even today, the debate continues about how a child learns to read. Reading is complex and requires the ability to pull together motor, perceptual and cognitive processes. As much as schools wanted students to develop reading skills in lockstep, children learn at different rates; they learn to read quickly or slowly, well or poorly, depending on who they are and how they are taught.

Yet America was founded on the concept of an informed and educated citizenry. For democracy to work, access to the printed word was essential. Reading not only gets people through work and everyday life, but facilitates the exchange of opinions, values and information that promotes the survival and evolution of a democratic culture. For a democracy to endure, all citizens, not just an aristocratic few, must be educated and informed to participate. This demanded the radical concept of educating the masses, beginning with reading.

Early American readers taught reading not as a process, but as a way to learn religious, rhetorical, moral and patriotic values. These books combined alphabets with Bible facts and verses. By the nineteenth century, readers were more likely to preach the golden rule and offer moral tales of honesty, obedience, temperance, thrift and patriotism. It wasn't until the early twentieth century that educators began to focus on the learner and not on society's precepts and values. For the first time, children were taught the "how" of reading, instead of the "what."

As the content and purpose of reading changed, so did the methods used to teach reading. Two basic techniques have been used since the nineteenth century: phonics, which is the ability to decode the printed word by recognizing letters and knowing the sound those letters stand for, and the whole word method, in which a child is taught to recognize entire words and their meaning at a glance. Educators' preferences used to swing between these two approaches, and it is only in the last few decades that a more holistic approach, which values both sound and words in context, has taken hold. Advocates of "pure" phonics believed that by learning to sound out words, children acquired the underlying skill to read any word they saw by matching it with its spoken equivalent. Whole word advocates maintained that children best learned to read by decoding the word as a whole unit, and understanding its meaning from its context. Current thinking favors the synthesis of sound/symbol relationships and the importance of understanding content in context.

Phonics, popular in the early nineteenth century, was challenged by the whole word method. It's interesting to note that Thomas Gallaudet's 1835 *Mother's Primer*, the first whole word book, included the lines, "Frank had a dog, his name was Spot…. Spot was a good dog." And educator Horace Mann protested in 1838, "eleven-twelfths of all the children in the reading classes did not understand the words they read so glibly," which was probably true, given the rhetoric and abstractness of their readers. He suggested the need for silent reading, with an emphasis on the meaning of words rather than on the sound of the letters.

The 1944 editorial team for Dick and Jane readers

As America shifted from a rural to an urban society and as waves of immigrants arrived, the mass education of these hordes of learners required a systematic approach to reading. McGuffey Readers, a series of five books graduated in difficulty, were introduced in 1836 and became the most widely used textbooks. Over a period of fifty years, 122 million copies reached classrooms. The readers were used to teach reading aloud, clearly and dramatically according to rules of rhetoric and oratory. These books stressed moral and religious issues such as the importance of family and respect for authority, patriotism and truthfulness. Gradually, other readers introduced restricted vocabulary and less abstract content.

At the turn of the century, inexpensive paper and high-volume printing techniques made it possible to mass produce readers, profusely illustrated with pictures mostly of children and animals. In 1897, Baldwin Readers, the first to use color pictures, became available. It wasn't until the 1930s that school surveys showed what educators suspected—that thousands of children were unable to read effectively. The monotonous memory drills of the nineteenth century had to be replaced with reading activities that freed children from the lockstep of traditional technique.

William S. Gray, an editor of the popular Elson Readers published by Scott Foresman, which featured stories about a family and its home life, conducted many of these early reading studies. In the process, he came up with a model for a new whole word reading system that evolved into Scott Foresman's innovative New Basic Reading Program. It was a system that deeply involved the teacher and would grow to include pre-primers, primers, workbooks, word cards and charts featuring two children named Dick and Jane, who from the 1930s through the 1960s taught millions of children how to read.

Jane's world; it's where she blossoms, where she measures her success and sees her accomplishments add up.

School is important too. Jane would never miss a day of class. She is a perfect student, carrying an armload of books, even if she's too young to read them. Jane is smart in the way little girls were supposed to be smart in the 1950s, when boys could be boys, but girls had to be girls. She is a young lady in training to be a perfect wife and mother. Jane is always calm, self-controlled and free of emotional extremes. No tantrums, no tears, no false moves. Jane is never a problem.

The Jane "Look"

In her forty-year career, Jane wore at least two hundred different ensembles. In story after story, whether Jane is dressed in dainty prints, solids or plaids, she always looks stylish. Jane never slouches, she stands up straight. She's a perfect model for her dresses with Peter Pan collars, jumpers, sweater and skirt sets, and party dresses with crinolines and fitted sashes. Since the illustrators who drew Dick and Jane wanted them to look familiar to readers, the outfits were based on clothing featured in Sears, Roebuck and Montgomery Ward mail order catalogs of the time. The ideal middle-class girl of the 1950s was ladylike and wore dresses everywhere, accessorized with hats, shoes, purses and clean white gloves to create a total "look."

Sears, Roebuck
Summer 1956 catalog

27

Sally

Sally is a force of nature, unpredictable and full of energy. What attracts her, she runs toward. Too young to play by the rules, Sally innocently barges through stories and into situations, spicing up Dick and Jane's life whenever she appears. If a story has a surprise ending, it's usually Sally's silly antics that make the plot spin. Sally is lucky enough to be the baby and gets away with mischief.

Sally walks through puddles in Mother's shoes, while Dick stands by laughing. She powders the noses of pets and toys alike, and everyone thinks she's cute. When she speeds down the street in her toy car, she's on her own, so focused and fearless in her determination to get where she wants, that she's oblivious to whatever might cross her path.

29

The Boom in Babyville

In the late 1940s, excited mothers and fathers-to-be, millions of them, were buying cribs and carriages and putting up circus wallpaper in nurseries all around the country. Optimistic about the future, these prospective parents were ready to have and cherish their children—seventy-six million American babies born in less than two decades. The baby boomers, as they've been called ever since, came in two tidal waves, the first from 1944 to 1949, the second between 1950 and 1957. *Fortune* magazine, in 1951, pronounced the baby boom "exhilarating.... A civilian market growing by the size of Iowa every year ought to be able to absorb whatever production the military will eventually turn loose." What got turned loose was a flood of postwar consumer goods, and parents across the nation did their share by mass-producing new consumers. The economy and the baby boom lunged forward together, for better and for worse.

When the first wave of babies entered school in the early fifties, the educational system strained and teachers and parents hit the panic button. The generation that was supposed to reap the benefits of America's postwar potential looked like it was going to be cheated out of a world-class education. Seventy-eight thousand makeshift classrooms were set up in vacant stores and churches. Three out of five classes were overcrowded, and forty-five children to a class was common. Students shared everything, including books and desks.

Parents demanded school expansion and new construction. They joined parent-teacher groups in record numbers (PTA membership doubled to eight million by 1952) to agitate for the supplies and reforms they wanted. Bond issues and higher local taxes raised the money for schools to expand. From 1950 to 1970, elementary school enrollment rose by two-thirds. In 1952, 50,000 new classrooms were built, but even that wasn't enough; in 1953, the average daily attendance rose by two million. By 1960, the federal government was spending $18 billion on elementary education, three times the amount spent a decade earlier. There was a staggering teacher shortage. Early in the fifties the country was 72,000 teachers short, and little had improved by 1959, when nearly one-tenth of the nation's 1.3 million teachers were working with substandard credentials.

Regardless of the quality of the educations they received, the baby boomers caused an unprecedented business bonanza. With 11,000 babies being born every day, businesses large and small had to accommodate the huge numbers of children who needed to be fed, clothed, educated and entertained. A *Life* magazine cover story in 1958 called the baby boom and the $33 billion juvenile market a "built-in recession cure." And it was. Each new consumer used up $800 worth of goods and services in the first year of its life: from baby food (1.5 billion cans a year, nationally) and diaper service ($50 million a year), to bronze baby shoes ($5 million a year to one company alone). Every dollar spent seemed like a good investment.

And, of course, there was television, which turned toddlers into a powerful consumer market. TV bypassed parents and appealed directly to kids, who soon learned to recognize brand names before they could read. They learned jingles before "The Star-spangled Banner." It was writer Joyce Maynard who observed, "We are, in the fullest sense, *consumers*, trained to salivate not at a bell, but at the sight of a Kellogg's label or a Dunkin' Donuts box." As they grew up, baby boomers' economic power turned their passing fads and fancies into major businesses. Whatever they did, they were a big and powerful group. Where the baby boomers went, the economy followed.

New supermarkets placed candy on shelves easy for little shoppers to reach.

No matter what she's up to, three-year-old Sally is always learning about the world. Everything that happens to her is new. She's the curious member of the family, free of responsibility and full of imagination. Sally struts, darts and responds to surprises with big theatrical gestures and a tiny vocabulary. Sally makes people pay attention to her, and she makes them laugh. She is so involved in the here and now, she can't think ahead. Sally is a magnet for mishaps. She loses Tim, her teddy bear, again and again. Sally drops her ice cream cone, gets lost on a bus and trapped under a big umbrella. Dick and Jane, who always watch out for her, don't mind, because they're responsible and eager to show Sally what it means to do the right thing. They never lose their patience or get too mad with Sally, because they remember that not so long ago, they were babies too.

Model Children

If Dick and Jane were Zerna Sharp's idea, it was Eleanor Campbell's illustrations that brought them to life. A popular Philadelphia illustrator, Campbell was the artist who defined the characters' looks and personalities and made them so convincing that first-graders counted them as friends. Campbell photographed real-life models—her relatives, friends and even neighborhood pets—who acted out the story lines and sketches Sharp and her editorial team developed. Working from snapshots, she was able to give the action in the stories their movie-like quality, and to capture the spontaneous energy of childhood.

Model for Jane

Models for Dick and Sally

Spot

"See Spot run," and he does. Hear Spot speak, "Bow-wow. Bow-wow." Like everyone else, he uses short words, repeated over and over. Dick and Jane and Sally understand Spot because he broadcasts whatever is on his mind. When he is happy to see someone, he smiles. When his ears fold back, he's in hot water, being chased by a chicken or attacked by a flying teddy bear. When Spot rolls his eyes up to the sky, he can't believe what he's gotten himself into.

Spot may be a dog, but he is featured in more stories than Mother and Father combined. That's because Spot wears two hats in Dick and Jane's world. Sure it's his job to make everyone laugh, but he also teaches Dick and Jane how to be responsible children. He can count on them to care for him every

day, to walk, groom and feed him. Spot has fun when he does his jobs too, greeting Father  at the front door, shaking hands with Grandfather when he arrives at the farm. If work is fun for Dick and Jane, it's a game for Spot, who rushes to bring in the laundry when it starts to rain.

Sometimes Spot suffers in silence, like the times Dick and Jane dress him up in human clothes or Sally powders him all over with Mother's makeup. Still, Spot maintains his dignity, even when the worst thing happens, when Dick longs for a new puppy. But most of the time, Spot will do anything to be part of the action. He swims, plays hide-and-seek, jumps rope (though not very well), even pulls the kids along on their skates. Good dog.

It is Spot's animal instincts that turn disasters into delight and make for more than a dog's share of happy endings. Time after time, Spot saves the day, finding the toy Sally drops overboard, buries in the sand or loses when she doesn't pay attention. You'd think he was a retriever. Spot first appeared in early Dick and Jane stories as a trim black-and-white terrier, because in the early 1930s, terriers were the most popular breed of dog. Spot turned into a sentimental cocker spaniel in 1936, when spaniels became best-selling dogs. But no matter what he looked like, kids loved Spot, because he reminded them of their pets at home and made every story more fun. Smart dog.

Puff

Puff is a soft, purring ball of fur, Jane and Sally's tiny orange kitten. Cute and cuddly, Puff is as frisky as Sally is curious. Pretty Puff, both civilized and brave, unties Mother's apron strings one day and plays fearlessly with barnyard animals the next. Silly Puff gets tangled in a big blue ball of yarn, trapped in a tree and sent on a harrowing swing ride.

It's a good thing Puff has nine lives. In a previous life—c.1930—she was known as Little Mew. With a new name, she became more adventurous. Puff steps in wet paint, chases and breaks balloons and is always knocking something off a table. But she is not bad. Puff never claws the furniture or picks fussily at her food or jumps up on the dining room table. Playing against type, Puff is not aloof. She'd never walk away from an affectionate pat. Puff even gets along with dogs—lucky Spot. Puff's rarely seen alone and seldom disappears to take a nap. Puff is a smarter cat than most and can jump rope a lot better than Spot. By the 1960s she's going for rides on Mother's modern vacuum cleaner and watching other cats on television.

34

Tim

Tim is the teddy bear, Sally's little sidekick who comforts her even though she treats him carelessly. In Dick and Jane's world, where only a few bad things happen, most of them happen to Tim, the good-natured pal. Tim never complains when Sally drags him wherever she goes, trailing him along the ground, dangling him sideways by an arm or upside down by his leg. In a non-speaking role, Tim can't scream for help when Sally sends him flying down the banister, where he collides with a startled Spot. Tim can't swallow when Sally force-feeds him water at the drinking fountain in the park. He can't budge when he's buried alive at a construction site. Tim can't swim when he slips over the rim of the little blue rowboat and nearly sponges up enough water to sink him forever. Tim may always need help, but it's really Sally who needs Tim. He's her playmate, her confidant, her little brother, her security blanket.

35

Fun with Dick & Jane

Every day is filled with fun in Dick and Jane's world. Every minute, every hour, someone's eyes are sparkling with delight. This is a family that likes to laugh. Everyone, even the  pets, knows the power of a smile, a giggle, a joke. To make reading fun, Dick and Jane's world has been turned into fun. Simple fun, inexpensive fun; you can tell that Mother and Father were children of the Depression. There are very few toys around the house, and all the kids share them: a ball, a wagon, a balsa-wood airplane, a few wooden blocks and some chalk. There are dolls, but none that talk, wet or walk. There's not a battery-operated toy in sight. Only a modest electric train set and a toy telephone. No one complains.

Full of energy like most little kids, Dick and Jane and Sally seldom sit still. They spend most of their time out of the house, out-of-doors, swimming, juggling, kite-flying, racing and throwing balls. In their backyard or on the front sidewalk, they run and jump and swing and slide. They ride bikes and ponies, play on the seesaw and swing from trees. They're pint-size acrobats. They can somersault, stand on their hands and still have energy left to horse around. Dick dangles from trees. Jane jumps rope and skates up a storm. Sally jumps up and down the stairs in the hallway and on the porch and, miraculously, never falls.

Dick and Jane don't count on Mother or Father to amuse them or to organize a game. They make their own fun. They play hide-and-seek, Simon says and blindman's bluff. Dick and Jane are creative. Their imaginations manufacture non-stop entertainment. They ride kitchen broomsticks as if they were frisky horses, turn the laundry basket into a boat and dress up in paper bags to look like scary ghosts.

Spot and Puff have fun too. Spot chases balls and butterflies and frogs, and loves to jump through the air to get his stick. Puff has a great time trying to catch a balloon and even more fun playing with Mother's ball of yarn. The kids have tea parties for the pets, play jokes on them and dress Puff up like a baby and make Spot pretty with Mother's face powder.

Toys Were Us

Fun got to be serious business in the decades following World War II. Toy sales in 1940 totaled only $84 million, but by the end of the 1950s, kids and parents and grandparents were spending $1.25 billion on everything from deluxe boxes of Crayolas to the first glamorous Barbie dolls. The market for toys was huge, but fickle. In December 1954, 40 million people saw Fess Parker as Davy Crockett on TV's *Disneyland*, and frenzied Americans spent more than $100 million on different Davy Crockett items—toothbrushes, snowsuits, coonskin caps, bathing suits, school lunch boxes, guitars and T-shirts—before the market collapsed in July 1955.

Silly Putty (1950) was World War II's gift to kids. This bouncing, stretchy rubber substitute was a pink blob best used to pick up, transfer and distort comic strip pictures. Mr. Potato Head (1952), the first toy advertised on television, was a box full of plastic ears, eyes, lips, mustaches, noses, hats and pipes that turned ordinary potatoes into the wackiest of characters. Chatty Cathy (1960) spoke eleven random phrases when a kid pulled her magic ring. "Tell me a story." "Please comb my hair." "I got hurt." "Where are we going?" "Change my dress," said the doll, who came either as a blue-eyed blonde or brown-eyed brunette.

NOTHING ELSE IS
Silly Putty®
Silly Putty
THE REAL SOLID LIQUID

Food is fun too. The kids devour vanilla ice cream cones whenever they have the chance. Mother and Grandmother bake them delicious layer cakes with white icing, big, round cookies and gingerbread men that the kids gobble up. Sally loves doughnuts, and Spot loves any crumb that falls his way.

Going places is as much fun as staying home. The kids climb the hill near their house and watch the cars on the highway zoom by. They enjoy window shopping with Mother and looking around in toy stores, bookshops and the grocery store. They pile in the car, excited about a trip to the zoo, the Fun Park or Grandmother and Grandfather's farm.

Wherever lighthearted Dick and Jane go, they take fun with them. Who wouldn't want to have them around? Dick and Jane and Sally know that life and everything about it—work, food, chores, school—is meant to be enjoyed. They're the kind of kids who fall asleep with smiles on their faces.

Father

Father is handsome. Father is young. Father is trim. Father is tall. Father has it all. He has a perfect family, a job that gets him home when it's light out and an even temperament that lets him take life one day at a time. Father adores Dick and Jane and Sally. Father loves Mother, the perfect wife and partner. Father, who never says a word about his job, is a breadwinner heading up the ladder of success, ready to do anything he can for his family. His family is his dream come true, and Father is happy.

Father and Mother raise their children together. Father always does his share. When Dick or Jane or Sally needs him, Father doesn't say, "I'm tired. Talk to your Mother." Father never says, "No." Father is fun-loving and energetic. Father is always on the go, fixing broken toys, washing the car, unpacking the new barbecue, building a birdhouse, planting shrubs in the garden. And still, there's energy to spare, to teach Dick to juggle, to jump rope with Jane, to carry Sally and Tim around on his shoulders. Father doesn't play favorites.

Gentle, tolerant, patient, soft-spoken, Father listens, like a modern, model father. No lectures about what the world was like when he was a kid. It is not Father's job to discipline or punish. It is not in his nature to be unfair, to withhold or act superior because he's older or because he's a man or because he's the husband or the father. No one has to call Father "Sir." He is a realist, not a romantic. Father is one of five citizens in a little democracy where everyone gets to be who he really is.

Every time Father strides up the walk to the front door in his business suit and hat, he steps into the safe world he shares with his family. At home, when Father smiles at everyone, everyone smiles back. That's one more reason for Father to be happy. For Father and the family, the big world and its problems never get through the white picket fence.

World War II infantry soldiers

Where's Poppa?
Many boys and girls weren't lucky enough to see their fathers as often as Dick and Jane saw theirs. During World War II, 1.24 million fathers left families behind to fight in Europe, Africa and the Pacific; many more had to leave to fight in the Korean War. Separated from them for years at a time, children grew up knowing their fathers through letters, snapshots and stories told around the kitchen table. By the end of the war, many fathers were dead, and other fathers came home wounded or emotionally scarred. The 1944 GI Bill of Rights encouraged close to eight million returning men to go back to school, with the government paying all costs for higher education and on-the-job training programs and a monthly living allowance of up to $120. Their goal? Land a job, climb the corporate ladder, buy homes and cars and braces for the kids and college educations and, years later, retire. If success demanded overtime and three-hour-a-day commutes, at least fathers saw their kids on weekends.

Park Forest, Illinois commuters heading home

Learning to Read with Dick and Jane

Why are Dick and Jane American icons? What makes us smile when we hear their names? Forty years of first-graders bonded with Dick and Jane, lived in their world and, through their adventures, learned to read. Teachers loved Dick and Jane because they did their job so well, and gave slow and smart kids alike the sequence of skills that turned them into successful readers. School boards chose Dick and Jane books because they were innovative products that got students on an organized learning track and moved them smoothly through the educational process.

Dick and Jane books were an educational breakthrough, the product of a decade of experimentation that fused the talents of educators, reading specialists, classroom teachers, child psychologists, writers and illustrators. The books set new standards in textbook publishing. They were easy to read, designed to be bright and attractive with their big color pictures and bold Century Schoolbook

anticipated what actions would happen next. They learned to interpret simple pictures, learn visual discrimination, recognize simple sentence patterns and practice eye-hand coordination. They also learned how to concentrate and pay attention, and to pick up social skills like working with other children and handling books properly.

William Gray and his associates pioneered the technique of "controlled vocabulary," in which a limited number of new words were introduced and then repeated at least ten times each until new readers learned to recognize them. In the paperbound pre-primers (*Dick and Jane; More Dick and Jane Stories; We Come and Go; We Look and See; We Work and Play; Sally, Dick and Jane; Fun with Our Family* and *Fun Wherever We Are*) and in primers (*Fun with Dick and Jane, New Fun with Dick and Jane* and *Fun with Our Friends*) and in the readers *Our New Friends* and *More Fun with Our Friends*, which were read in the second half of first grade, words printed with the illustrations were the spoken words of the charac-

The 1956 *Before We Read*

We Work and Play

New Fun with Dick and Jane

Think-and-Do workbook

typeface. The stories were short and upbeat, shunning the abstraction, gloom and monotony of earlier readers. Simple sentence structure and limited vocabulary helped kids learn quickly. The whole word or "look-say" method was based on the goal of teaching a student to recognize the form of a word and then to understand its meaning in the context of its use. Teachers also used phonics in every lesson, sounding out letters and letter combinations to reinforce word recognition.

Scott, Foresman and Company's Curriculum Foundation Series was a textbook program that moved students from kindergarten through eighth grade. It was only for the first months of the first grade that Dick and Jane appeared in reading readiness books, pre-primers, a primer, a workbook, on word cards, as cutouts and in oversize Big Books. But they were such unforgettable characters, they made a lasting impression. By the first half of the second grade, however, kids said good-bye to Dick and Jane, who subsequently appeared only in a few stories in readers that introduced a new cast of characters and more difficult stories.

In the 1930s and '40s, reading readiness was a new concept that taught pre-reading skills by getting students to pay attention to the content of pictures. Children looked at the pictures in *Before We Read*—and later, in the 1950s, in *We Read Pictures* and *We Read More Pictures*—and described what characters were saying, then

ters. Children learned to transfer the meaning of a spoken word to its printed form. When children in the 1950s finished reading three pre-primers, they could recognize fifty-eight new words.

When the teacher first passed the primer *Fun with Dick and Jane* down classroom aisles, kids felt that they were finally holding their first "real" book. Clothbound and filled with more words, the stories were longer and presented more complicated ideas than pre-primers. The settings for stories took Dick and Jane out into the world, to the farm, to town, to the zoo and to activities that included a widening circle of friends. Each student was given a *Think-and-Do Book*. These workbooks were filled with visual discrimination and reading exercises that children completed on their own.

The Dick and Jane system was meant to be comprehensive, with enough built-in steps from pre-literacy to literacy to insure that children got all the skills they needed to read. Teacher's Editions made the teacher's job easier. Books were periodically updated. Trained reading specialists traveled around the country to visit teachers and observe how materials were being used and to comment on what worked and what didn't. Every five years, based on specialists' input and requests from state school boards, stories were revised and illustrations updated. The revisions reflected changes in clothing, household furnishings, automobiles and, by the 1960s, the physical and psychological sophistication of children.

Mother

Mother is pretty. Mother is graceful. Mother is mellow and Mother is smart. She knows how to do it all: be a good partner to Father, a nurturing Mother to Dick and Jane and Sally and an effortless homemaker, who makes everything look easy. Mother makes the American Dream happen. Mother sews. Mother launders. Mother cooks. Mother sweeps. Mother knits. Mother walks to town to shop. Somehow, every day, Mother must get her work done: washing dishes, cooking meals, ironing, and washing floors and windows. Mother is happy when the house looks neat and beautiful. Her family doesn't just function, it thrives. That makes Mother happiest of all.

Mother likes to look good and dresses like a lady. She wears hats and gloves and pretty soft day dresses. She has pretty pocketbooks for every occasion. Mother is feminine and sits with ankles crossed and hands clasped. Mother has poise and seems to glide as she walks. No sharp turns, no sudden movements. Even when she jumps rope, Mother has style.

Mother is easy-going. She doesn't hover, doesn't have to check up on Dick or Jane or Sally to see what they're doing, to know that they're OK. Mother trusts Dick and Jane, and trusts them to watch out for Sally. There's no need to lecture or order anyone around. Mother is proud of her efficient, winning team.

Mother's life has no frustrations or setbacks. Just outside the world of Dick and Jane, the new suburban mothers were excited about their new homes and their new families too. But many whirled like spinning tops from one role to the next—maid, cook, chauffeur, referee, cheerleader, romantic partner and ego booster. Many women had jobs and still got a hot dinner on the table.

And many more did not live in the suburbs or enjoy the benefits of the postwar boom.

Dick and Jane's Mother doesn't have an outside-the-home job. She works at home all day and when everything's done sits in her chair, not a hair out of place, reading magazines. Mother is a modern miracle. She teaches quietly, by example. She's cool and doesn't yell and never, never nags or corrects. Mother is selfless, soothing and approving. Mother may be young, but she's wise. Like a Buddha, smiling Mother embraces Dick and Jane and Sally and Father and her world for all it is.

Changing Role of Women

If Dick and Jane's mother took pride in her secure and tranquil married life, other women were not so sure. The novelist Pearl S. Buck, in her 1941 book, *Of Men and Women*, described her observations of a prosperous American housewife's day: "She listens to as much as they will tell her, she reads as much as she is inclined, she potters about on the fringes of the world which really goes on without her and comforts herself by having a good hot dinner ready at night anyway. It is not enough." By the end of the fifties, a growing number of women were starting to feel the same way—confused about their traditional roles as wives and mothers and frustrated by their limited options.

In the 1930s, movie audiences applauded and Oscars were awarded to actresses who played tough women making their way in a tough world. The country needed role models who could withstand adversity. With the onset of World War II, millions of women said good-bye to their husbands who went off to war, and took control of their households, often leaving their children with neighbors or family to take over a man's job. The independence some women had longed for was finally theirs. During the war years, more than one-third of the civilian labor force was female, and more than three-quarters of them were married. Between 1941 and 1945, women earned $8 billion and felt the thrill of having, spending and saving their own money. Conventional wisdom might still proclaim that a woman's first allegiance was to home and children. But the truth was that once the war was over, many women didn't want to go home and many simply did not want to give up their financial freedom. Two-thirds of them did not give up working.

It wasn't easy managing a job and a home, or giving back good jobs to returning veterans to take lesser jobs for lesser pay, but the women who stuck it out wouldn't turn back. And society went along with their limited ambitions. As long as women didn't confuse a job with a career, no one could disapprove. Their money made a difference; it helped pay off the new mortgage, was banked for a kid's college tuition or splurged on a vacation.

Suburban women who didn't have jobs may have found themselves with everything they could want, but they were isolated from their mothers, sisters and old friends. Without any on-the-job training, they scoured advice-filled women's magazines on

In the 1930s, the majority of states had laws prohibiting the employment of married women; by 1960, ten million wives were working.

supermarket lines and at home to figure out their changing role in a changing world. How to be an attractive wife, a devoted mother, an optimistic and efficient manager? Magazines like *McCall's*, *Ladies Home Journal*, *Family Circle*, *Woman's Day* and *Redbook* provided road maps to fulfillment, recipes, homemaking tips, ads and editorials that either idolized or chastised women who felt responsible for everything and answerable to everyone. Articles instructed women what to eat, how to dress, how to live and, most importantly, how happiness was to be measured.

The ideal of a fulfilled woman at the helm of a child-centered nuclear family had its heyday for a short time, from the first blush of the postwar boom until the mid-1950s. By 1956, *Life* magazine reported on "Changing Roles in Modern Marriage:" "If there is such a thing as a 'suburban syndrome' it might take this form: the wife, having worked before marriage, or at least having been educated and socially conditioned toward the idea that work… carries prestige," might become depressed about being a mere housewife. Even if she avoids this, "her humiliation still seeks an outlet. This may take various forms: in destructive gossip about other women, in raising hell at the PTA, in becoming a dominating mother."

Despite the decade's glorification of domesticity and togetherness, there was a growing gap between smiling home-all-day wives and the reality of everyday family life. While wives were supposed to take pride in redecorating their houses, volunteering for library work and making home an oasis for a harried husband, these activities couldn't paper over gnawing frustrations and genuine discontent. Tranquilizer and liquor sales were rising, and so were the divorce rates.

Women who were better educated and looking forward to longer lives felt a jolt of recognition when, in 1963, they read Betty Friedan's *The Feminine Mystique*: "It was a strange stirring, a sense of dissatisfaction, a yearning that women suffered in the middle of the twentieth century in the United States. Each suburban wife struggled with it alone. As she made the beds, shopped for groceries, matched slipcover materials, ate peanut butter sandwiches with her children, chauffeured Cub Scouts and Brownies, lay beside her husband at night, she was afraid to ask even of herself the silent question—'Is this all?' "

The Family

Dick, Jane and Sally Who? They have no last name, but it doesn't matter. Family matters. A fun-loving, secure family, where everyone plays and nobody yells. A happy family, where the kids are free to be kids and are so good that Mother and Father never say no. A traditional family, with a pretty Mother, a handsome Father, two kind and generous Grandparents, three well-adjusted kids (not too many, not too few), and a menagerie of equally well-adjusted pets. A family where everyone is trusting and shares a sense of humor, the kind of family every child, and every parent, wants.

 In the world of Dick and Jane, children get more attention than adults. Self-sufficient Dick and Jane make no great demands. Mother and Father are ready to approve, to

play, to fix things, to amuse. Their job is easy. They don't have to discipline or punish, because none of their children steps out of line. Dick and Jane don't cry, because bad things don't happen to them. Dick and Jane don't tattle, because there's nothing to tattle about. Their family lives in harmony, in a universe all its own. There are no uncles, aunts or cousins. No arguments, no competition, no power plays. No fighting. No secrets.

The nuclear family is a tight-knit, winning team because each member is loved and respected for who he is and what he can do. This is a family that wants to be together, around the dining room table, playing out in the yard and when they climb in the car to go visiting. No one wants or needs to be alone, because they enjoy each other's company so much. Everyone communicates well. Things don't get fussed over, they get done. Mother and Father watch and listen. It's their job to pay attention to the kids, to care. And it works. Dick and Jane and Sally feel so secure, so wanted, so loved, that parents don't need to say, "Good boy," "Good girl," "You're smart," "You're pretty." "I love you."

As Seen on TV

After reading about Dick and Jane's family during the school day, kids came home and after dinner many sat side by side with their mothers and fathers, watching television. Popular situation comedies, staples of 1950s programming, featured ideal families—understanding fathers who never work and wise and wily mothers who managed happy homes. On these long-running shows, season after season, well-behaved children grew up before America's eyes. These perfect families, watched so loyally, felt like neighbors and were looked up to as role models.

Ozzie and Harriet (1952-66)   *Father Knows Best (1954-62)*   *The Donna Reed Show (1958-66)*

Grandparents

Grandmother and Grandfather are the oldest people in Dick and Jane's world. They may not jump rope or crawl under chairs to play follow the leader, but they have as much enthusiasm and energy as Mother and Father. Grandmother and Grandfather live on a farm, far away from Dick and Jane. When they visit Dick and Jane's house to celebrate birthdays, they always bring nice presents and are fun to be with. On the farm, where Grandmother and Grandfather are always busy, they enjoy what they do. They spend their days planting their fields and tending the animals. Grandmother bakes delicious cookies and scrumptious birthday cakes. Grandfather wants Dick and Jane and Sally to learn how farm animals live. He encourages them to try new things, to take risks, to explore. Grandfather cheers the kids on when they race the pony. On every visit to Grandmother and

Grandfather's farm, something exciting happens.

In the 1960s, Dick and Jane's Grandmother and Grandfather looked and felt a lot younger than their peers of a generation earlier. America was getting younger, and Grandmother and Grandfather moved with the flow. They gave up their spectacles, got flattering new hairstyles, started wearing denim clothes and looked a lot younger too. Out on city streets, young people were shouting, "Don't trust anyone over thirty," but Grandmother and Grandfather were still getting the respect they deserved. Even Spot could tell they were special, and as

soon as the car door would open, he'd jump out, stand up, and stick out his paw to shake hands.

Good Morning, Class! Since the nineteenth century, the teaching of children has been considered "women's work." Children went from their mother's care to the care of a female teacher, usually a local woman who trained at a "normal school," as two-year teacher training colleges were then called. Teachers were idealistic but practical women who generally embraced their profession with intensity and dedication. For generations, teaching was one of the very few respectable ways for an unmarried woman to make a living. The stereotypical teacher was a strict disciplinarian who taught by the rules, drilling kids in reading, writing and arithmetic as she paced the aisles and kept up the pace by clapping. After World War II, more men entered the profession, and by 1960 there were an equal number of men teaching, but only at the high school level.

51

On the Farm

A trip to Grandmother and Grandfather's farm is a special treat. The farm is a beautiful place. Dick and Jane's Mother, or maybe it was Father, grew up here. There are big green meadows and taller trees than Dick and Jane have in their backyard. There's a farmhouse, a chicken coop, a red barn and a stable for the horses and ponies. The animals that live on the farm are not pets. Each one has a job to do—horses work, dogs round up animals, cats catch pesky mice.

The farm is where Dick and Jane learn that milk comes from cows, not bottles, that eggs come from hens, not cartons in the market. Grandfather and Grandmother work with their hands and, watching and helping

them, Dick and Jane share in the fun of their accomplishments. It's in the darkness of the barn, discovering a cat with her newborn kittens, that Dick and Jane are reminded by Grandfather about how important families are. On the farm, they learn about self-reliance and see how everyone has to work together, people and animals too.

It's on the farm that Dick and Jane are introduced to farm values and a bigger view of nature. Playing under big old trees; running through grass and not on side-walks; riding on real horses, not on broom-sticks; the farm is far away and very different from Dick and Jane's modern everyday lives.

2. Living the A

merican Dream

By the early 1950s—after nearly twenty years of fine-tuning reading techniques, stories and graphics—Dick and Jane books had hit their stride. Educational theory, content and form were all in sync, a dependable way to teach reading, a system that worked for the market it targeted. The safe, colorful and fun world of Dick and Jane and Sally permeated the lives of millions of children, as the basal series became the most widely used reading program in the history of American education. Children recognized that the seamless world they saw in the books—a place where no need went unanswered, where unhappiness, trouble and fear existed someplace else, far away—would be a great world to live in and a great place to be a child.

The American Dream that promised the postwar generation a storybook world was becoming a reality, put in place bit by bit by businessmen, politicians, the media and millions of enthusiastic new parents. The speed and efficiency that won the war now produced instant homogenized communities, full of tract homes that were promoted as individual little worlds with rooms and closets to fill. People lived next door to people pretty much like themselves, neighbors bound not by friend-ship or family but by ambition, newly achieved status and shared beliefs and fears. A 1954 *McCall's* magazine picture story endorsed family "togetherness"—working as a team—as one way to claim and enjoy the payoff for two decades of trouble and sacrifice.

Inexperienced suburbanites turned to all sorts of experts for advice. But the expert with the biggest impact was Dr. Benjamin Spock, whose *Common Sense Book of Baby and Child Care* (1946) was the best-selling guide to child-rearing that comforted parents so they could comfort their children. Spock wrote, "You know more than you think you do." Even so, parents placed their trust in Spock's comprehensive index, which walked them, step by step, through tantrums and toilet training.

For the first time in a long time, people had options. Wartime materials, recycled as new products with high-tech names, were put to imaginative uses. Polyethylene, once used as electrical insulation, was molded into Tupperware. The small cathode ray tubes that guided bombers now made television sets cheaper to produce and radios small enough to fit in a pocket. Polystyrene, used for life preservers, was shaped into Styrofoam coffee cups. America, retooled, was back on track.

A multitude of choices encouraged people to create their own postwar life-styles. Early American living room. Traditional bedroom. Modern kitchen. Luxurious, stain-free carpets in every color. Loosely woven Fiberglas drapes that swayed in the breeze. Nubby sectional sofa parts were designed to be rearranged—moved opposite the fireplace, nearer the television set or facing one another to stimulate conversation at cocktail parties.

Technology continually improved on nature. Families could enjoy "fresh" fruit cocktail and frozen Florida orange juice, all year long. TV dinners delivered effortless Thanksgiving feasts of turkey with all the trimmings any day of the week. Cakes rose from foolproof mixes. Fluffy Minute Rice cooked "instantly." Cheese spread. Ketchup flowed. Jell-O was sculpted, and dehydrated onion soup mixes transformed sour cream into party dip. Vitamin-enriched milk and Wonder Bread helped fill a child's daily nutritional needs, and the endless choices of multi-shaped and multi-colored breakfast

cereals made those same children vocal connoisseurs to be reckoned with at the cash register.

There was always one "last" consumer choice to make before life would be perfect. Once the first wave of appliances was bought—frost-free refrigerators, automatic washing machines, electric ranges—housewives moved on to a second tier of steam irons, pressure cookers, Mixmasters, electric blankets and vacuum cleaners with attachments that reached into every corner and crevice. With so many labor-saving devices, women were driven to higher standards of housekeeping perfection and actually spent more time cleaning the house than ever before.

Anyone looking through the picture window could see neighbors wearing the same clothes and doing the same things—planting flowering shrubs, squirting lighter fluid on charcoal briquettes, washing the car, and late at night dragging noisy aluminum garbage cans out to the curb. Men weeded and mowed so their lawns blended into one yard-to-yard green carpet that stretched uninterrupted all the way

1950

The more suburbia sprawled, the more cars became central to an American way of life. Car registration soared from 26 million in 1945 to 40 million in 1950 to 60 million by 1959. When the first baby boomers got their driver's licenses, the number exploded to 88 million.

Packaging was intensely studied in the 1950s by manufacturers and consumers alike. Stodgy labels were updated by industrial designers who aimed to communicate images that would sell as well on the small television screen as from the supermarket shelf.

By 1950, 1.4 million new homes had been built to accommodate first-time home buyers, returning war veterans and their new families. They visited model homes and selected payment options, floor plans and appliances from builders' brochures. From 1950 to 1960, the number of new homeowners rose from 23.6 million to 32.8 million people.

Dwight D. Eisenhower, President from 1952 to 1960, was a plain speaker with an honest face that voters liked. His record as commander of all Allied forces in WWII and his pledge to work for peace during the Korean War won him the 1952 election.

The American Dream had promised

down the street. Entertained and diverted by life's new choices, one choice most people didn't make was to step out of line. Like teams of synchronized swimmers, the smiling American men and women who most benefited from the pursuit of the American Dream also conformed to its ground rules. Husbands went to jobs and came home, like clockwork. Wives cooked and cleaned, then read magazines about how to cook and clean better. Kids lived by the clock too, and went to school, and after school were shuttled to dance classes, scout meetings and Little League games.

Everyone climbed into the car, then out, back and forth on excursions to the outside world. Drive to the station and catch the train to work. Drive to the brightly lit supermarket and survey the alluring packages lined up on metal-edged shelves, or piled deep in finger-numbing freezers. Drive to church. Drive back to the old neighborhood to visit relatives who didn't choose a new life, or didn't have the option. Drive for the fun of driving. To buy an ice cream cone. To go to the beach, a drive-in, an amusement park. Once a year, take a long drive to another state and vacation for a while. Then come home to find that your neighbor had watered the lawn and that everything else was exactly where you'd left it.

At first, suburban life in the 1950s seemed as alluring as a Technicolor movie. The plot was simple: live the American Dream, count on progress without too much pain. New lines of dialogue were written and delivered every day, in newspapers and magazines like *Life* and *Look*. Advertisements, everywhere, stirred desire, defined glamour and accelerated the plot. Buy this! Buy that! Look like him! Be like her! Cash registers rang. Then television changed American life, upping the ante, broadcasting messages morning till night. Hour-long dramas, reinforcing American values, mesmerized the family. Half-hour sitcoms let viewers laugh as they measured the private lives they were living against the small-screen fictional lives they were watching. Some experiences didn't match. But in a suburban culture obsessed with the way things looked, what you couldn't relate to didn't matter.

Then people began to realize that their world was developing cracks. Politicians and increasingly persuasive "media" barraged them about circumstances literally beyond their control. So working even harder together, nuclear families did their best to avoid anything or anyone who might spoil their perfect world—from neighbors of other races, to juvenile delinquents,

Every Saturday and for fifty cents, kids spent the afternoon watching double and triple bill shows, which changed weekly at local movie theaters. Color movies became commonplace in the 1950s, and special techniques like Cinemascope and 3-D tried to lure audiences away from television.

Twenty million Americans watched the Army-McCarthy hearings on television starting in 1950, when Republican Senator Joseph R. McCarthy launched a four-year binge of character assassination. He charged government leaders and cultural figures with a range of offenses, from sympathizing with communists to being committed members of the Communist Party.

the postwar generation a storybook world. Now,

to communists. People shunned, swept under the carpet or repressed any behavior that fell outside the norm, anything "deviant" or weird. The nuclear family was an exaggeration of family harmony, just as domesticity in the 1950s was exaggerated, with its matching stoves, dishwashers, clothes dryers, refrigerators, dish towels and pot holders. The harmony was as much a function of isolationism as it was of togetherness.

A-bombs had won the war. American nuclear power promised to transform the future, but Americans had been nervous since Russia tested its atomic bomb in 1949. At any time, a cold war could turn hot, as people learned when the Korean War broke out in 1950. America's postwar sense of security turned out to be short-lived. People were scared, and the dangers of the time were hard for kids to understand. Why did parents keep watching the scowling face of Senator Joseph McCarthy on TV? Why didn't they like how Elvis Presley sang or the way he danced? Why did soldiers with

guns have to walk with black children when they went to school? Why did some kids get polio and others not? Cold war fears seeped through schoolroom windows when alarms rang. Kids crouched in hallways or crawled under desks, covering their heads as they waited for the building to collapse. What would happen if they lived and their parents died? "Duck and cover!" wasn't fun, like a fire drill.

Sexual Behavior in the Human Male and *Sexual Behavior in the Human Female*, Alfred Kinsey's controversial books, exposed the unspoken realities of Americans' sex lives. Sending shock waves through the bedrooms of suburbia, Kinsey's explicit book about women's sex lives caused such an uproar that TV evangelist Billy Graham admonished, "It is impossible to estimate the damage this book will do to the already deteriorating morals of America." American educators were jolted, four years later, when the communists launched Sputnik in 1957. Political leaders and teachers alike feared that the country's "good times" mentality was doing the country in.

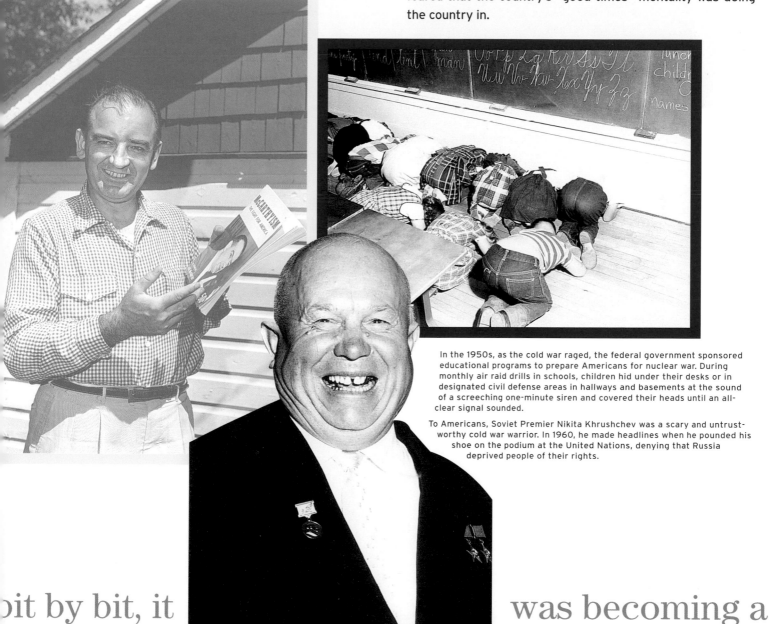

In the 1950s, as the cold war raged, the federal government sponsored educational programs to prepare Americans for nuclear war. During monthly air raid drills in schools, children hid under their desks or in designated civil defense areas in hallways and basements at the sound of a screeching one-minute siren and covered their heads until an all-clear signal sounded.

To Americans, Soviet Premier Nikita Khrushchev was a scary and untrustworthy cold war warrior. In 1960, he made headlines when he pounded his shoe on the podium at the United Nations, denying that Russia deprived people of their rights.

bit by bit, it   was becoming a

The tension between the perfect material world the middle class was working so hard to maintain and the uncontrollable forces of history were bound to rub the gloss off America's postwar fantasy. Day after day, while over a third of America's women were working outside their homes, others were depressed and downed record numbers of tranquilizers to keep their lives intact. Men's seeming willingness to trade in conscience for money and a "gray flannel" suit made them feel trapped even if they did spend all weekend trying to be good fathers and husbands. The more people wanted, the more people had to juggle, and the more fragile the "good life" began to feel.

It is not surprising that as traditional beliefs eroded in the late fifties, people tried all kinds of things to keep their own lives under control. More Americans went to church than ever before, to be comforted by a spirituality they hoped would transcend current events and the stress that sometimes kept them awake at night. Science fiction movies about aliens who "passed" as humans and television shows that went forward and backward in time took some of the edge off people's anxieties. It was comforting to think that the bad world existed outside one's own. Children and adults alike spent more and more of their leisure time re-creating trouble-free worlds that were a hallmark of the 1950s. They played miniature golf and filled in paint-by-number sets. Kids mailed away for ant farms, rearranged miniature furniture in split-level dollhouses, reconfigured electric train sets. Families passed around View-Master slides, and switched from one seamless world to the next on TV.

This theme-park ride of mid-century life, when the American Dream seemed to be within the reach of most middle-class families, felt like it could go on forever. Until the mid-1960s, when long-ignored demands for equal rights and opportunities for minorities would change the political and social fabric of America, the surface of this synthetic suburban world paralleled the candy-colored world of Dick and Jane. These worlds looked alike and each reflected what the majority of American consumers wanted. But America was changing, and no picket fence was tall enough, no driveway long enough, no big city far enough away to insulate the people lucky enough to be living the American Dream from change.

reality, and it felt like it could go on forever.

The August 15, 1959, cover of *The Saturday Evening Post* summed up what newlyweds were dreaming about in the 1950s: a house, cars, limitless appliances and power tools, a swimming pool.

At Home

"Ding dong!" the doorbell chimes. The screen door slams. Welcome to Dick and Jane's house, where no room has four walls or any corners. Home is an evocative stage set, with just enough familiar touches to convey a sense of well-being and comfort. There are many doorways for Dick and Jane and Sally to run in and out of, and few rugs to trip on. It's a home with just enough hints of style—patches of homey wallpaper and cheery curtains, a random chair or piece of furniture—to let you know that Mother and Father are solidly middle-class.

Even though we're never exactly sure just what kind of neighborhood Dick and Jane live in, we know

they're lucky, because they don't live in the city. And they don't have to share a house with Grandmother and Grandfather. Dick and Jane have what everybody dreams of—their own rooms in their own house.

Dick and Jane live in a traditional house. Everything in it is supposed to feel familiar and typical. There's a living room that's seldom used, a dining room the family eats in every day, and Mother's busy kitchen. A front hall leads to a staircase to the second floor, where there are at least three bedrooms but maybe only one bathroom. Father has his workshop in the basement. It's not a modern home, like a lot of new houses in the 1950s. There are no kidney-shaped tables, no blond-wood furniture, Corning Ware, Tupperware or harvest gold kitchen appliances. There's not even a record player or a radio. There is no barbecue in the backyard or television in the living room until the 1960s. But it's a comfortable house, bright and airy, where kids can do pretty much what they want. No plastic slipcovers protect the furniture, but well-behaved Dick and Jane know enough to keep their feet off the couch. Sally might not. And Spot and Puff? The opportunity never arises.

Building Blocks

More than one million acres of farmland were plowed under every year during the 1950s to make room for new houses for new families. The American Dream was finally an affordable reality for families who made around $3,000 a year and had never been able to afford a home before. All they had to do was make a $58 down payment and move into their mortgaged house as soon as the painters moved out. Of thirteen million homes built between 1948 and 1958, eleven million were built in the suburbs, which were growing fifteen times faster than any other part of the country. For the first time—using their savings, government loans and mortgages—more Americans owned homes than rented them. It was a new life-style that called for new schools, new churches and new swimming pools.

Nobody built houses faster than William J. Levitt, whose Levittown development in Hempstead, New York, defined suburbia as a place to live, a way of life with its own rules: no fences, no "Negro" families, no laundry hanging on clotheslines. Between 1947 and 1951, Levitt built and immediately sold 17,311 nearly identical Cape Cod and ranch-style homes. It was reported that on one day, he closed on 1,100 homes in five hours. At a price of between $7,770 and $9,500, the profit for each unit averaged $1,000. Using nails and lumber manufactured by Levitt, trained teams of workmen built houses in twenty-seven orderly steps. On a good day, thirty-six houses could be completed.

Built on a concrete slab, each house, with its pitched roof and louvered shutters, sat on a generous 60 X 100-foot plot (2,000 feet more than required by law). The small four-room dwelling had two bedrooms, one bath, a 12 X 16-foot living room and a modern kitchen. Landscaping, including four fruit trees, and all kitchen appliances were included. Some houses even came with a built-in television set and a Bendix washing machine as incentives.

Early Levittown kitchens shared the front of the house with the living room, in an open plan that turned the kitchen into the nerve center of the house. Life was more informal, less traditional. Seventy percent of meals were now eaten in the kitchen. The kitchen was the dining room, the laundry room and the "real" living room, where cooking, socializing and other household chores previously done in

Even when they were closed to the public, Levittown's model homes lured young couples to glimpse a new life-style.

private were now semipublic. The housewife-mother stood center stage in her kitchen, no longer relegated to the background.

Bathrooms were a third of the size they had been in turn-of-the-century houses. Bedrooms were big enough for a bed and a few pieces of furniture. This lack of space reinforced the "togetherness" being lauded in magazines and pushed people out the back door once the weather got warm. The backyard was the biggest room in the house, a place to barbecue, to cool off in the aboveground pool, play badminton and relax on the patio furniture. Fired up with a do-it-yourself mentality, the young men of suburbia mowed lawns, finished basements and repainted furniture. Levitt once joked, "No man who owns his own house and lot can be a communist. He has too much to do."

Parents moved to suburbia for peace and quiet and fresh air for their children. Kids played unsupervised with kids their own age on safe streets and cul-de-sacs. Parents wanted to shield their children from what they considered to be harmful influences, to make sure their children grew up according to their own standards, and not somebody else's. Most of the tensions in suburbia centered around children—how to discipline them, how to achieve quality in their schools, how to promote or ignore the class differences that distinguished one family from another.

Not everyone found suburbia to be a new Eden. Social critics lamented the loss of individualism, worried about the isolation of women and children and the domestication of men. They feared that traditional roles would get distorted, with women turned into overbearing wives and mothers. Men, they cautioned, would appear as overnight guests in their own homes, and children would be spoiled and delinquent. But while critics railed, the most important studies of Levittown showed that while some people were dissatisfied, especially women who missed the families they left behind, Levittowners talked frequently to their relatives on the telephone and visited them often, but did not want to move back to crowded, pressured cities.

The suburb became such a symbol of the American way of life that when Soviet Premier Nikita Khrushchev paid his first visit to America in 1959, President Eisenhower wanted him to visit Levittown to see the American Dream firsthand. Mr. Khrushchev declined.

Backyard Fun

The air is fresh, and the sun always shines. New white picket fences and old, tall, leafy trees mark the edges of Dick and Jane's outdoor domain. In front and back yards, the well-watered grass is very green. It smells good. No weeds, brown spots, bare patches, no dandelions mar the smooth, flat lawn. Everything Dick and Jane see belongs to them in this little utopia, where butterflies float between blossoms, flowers bloom in the garden, and Spot and Puff feel most at home.

Dick and Jane, who spend most of their time outside the house, are lucky that they're left on their own, unsupervised. The backyard is a safe place. No one has to watch them. They play by themselves, and sometimes with friends Susan, Pete and Billy, in their little suburban Arcadia, where it never snows, barely rains and never gets dark. After all, that's why Mother and Father moved here, to the "country," to be a little bit closer to nature. The backyard is Dick and Jane's private landscape, the place to do somersaults, fly a kite or toy plane, take a giant step, test out stilts,

swing from strong branches, roll in piles of red and yellow autumn leaves. The fun ends only when Mother stands in the screen door, calling "Diiiiiiick!" "Jaaaaaane!" and it's time to go back inside.

Mother and Father like to be outside as much as they can too. Father mows the lawn and washes the car. Mother hangs up laundry to dry, then takes it down. Everyone works in the garden. Spot digs holes, chases frogs and plays hide-and-seek. When Puff climbs a tree, she can count on being rescued. Tim likes to be out-of-doors too, even if all he does is sit on the back steps, watching everyone else have fun.

Family Values

Big gold stars for Dick and Jane, who behave so well. "Do unto others as you would have others do unto you," says the Golden Rule. And Dick and Jane do. They've learned their lessons well. Where? At home. How? By listening carefully, by trusting and respecting Mother and Father. Why? Dick and Jane are encouraged to say what they mean, and when they speak, people listen. The children are respected for what they think and who they are.

Dick and Jane live in a world where only good exists. They don't hang around with kids who set bad examples. There are no bad influences, no comic books, TV shows or movies. No one in their little world competes or cheats. No one snitches, no one teases and no one ever lies.

Dick and Jane know how to share. They share toys, they share problems, they share fun. Dick and Jane know what it means to be responsible. They take care of Spot and Puff. They take care of their bikes and skates and wagon. They help around the house. Dick and Jane are always polite and well-behaved. They shake hands with their elders, they never talk back or grab things, and they always wait their turn.

But what Dick and Jane and everyone around them knows best is the value of work. "Work. Work. Work," says Sally as she watches a steam shovel in action. "I can work," says Dick as he helps Jane set the table. "I can work," says Jane as she makes a yellow dress for her doll. Mother does housework with a smile on her face. Father, home from work, fixes anything

Lessons to Learn

School is a place where values are passed along. But what values get passed along depends on when, where and how you live. At the peak of Dick and Jane's success, the books—short on vocabulary—were long on traditional American values. Here are some big moral lessons reinforced in these little readers.

Respect your parents	Appreciate nature
Help your siblings	Be proud of your accomplishments
Families have fun when they work together	Behave in the car and on the bus
Cooperate	Work and play well with others
Play is valuable	
Use your imagination	The older you are, the more you should do
Don't complain	
Be kind to animals	Take school seriously
Help others	Cleverness is rewarded
Be enthusiastic	Clean up after yourself
Take chances	
Be considerate	Follow directions and rules
Share what you have	Ask permission when you're in doubt
Amuse yourself	
Be like your parents	Watch out for the safety of others
Be curious	
Work hard at your job	Accept other people's limitations
Mind your manners	
Be creative	Be nice to people
All people are equal	Encourage others
Be self-assured	Keep your sense of humor
Express what you feel	Reading is good

at the drop of a hat. Jane gardens happily. Dick has fun watering the lawn and feeding Spot. Spot works to find Tim, and Sally plays by making believe she's working.

Work is the eighteenth new word in the Dick and Jane vocabulary. Most of the people Dick and Jane meet work, and work happily. The milkman comes to the house as he has for years, cheery and efficient, dropping off milk and cream in glass bottles with paper lids, and picking up the empties. Mother is glad to see the dry cleaner who comes right up to the front door, with arms full of dresses, bedspreads and the curtains Mother can't wash in the new washing machine. People do their jobs well, and Dick and Jane are happy to see them because they make Mother's work just a bit easier.

Who Wants a Toy?

"See the toys," said Sally.

"Horses and cows and pigs!
And a funny red duck!
I want that funny red duck."

"Oh, Sally," said Dick.
"You have a yellow toy duck.
Do you want a red duck, too?"

"Oh, I guess not," said Sally.

74

"See that baby doll," said Jane.
"That doll can talk.
I want it.
I want a doll that talks."

"Oh, Jane," said Dick.
"You have two big dolls.
Do you want a baby doll, too?"

"Oh, I guess not," said Jane.
"I guess I have all the dolls
I want."

75

Two Moral Tales

Two Moral Tales Impressionable children don't learn values only at home, they pick up information and cues everywhere they go, from the movies to Sunday school. They learn what's important, how to behave and how to tell right from wrong. Traditionally, American reading books have advocated religion and patriotism. The educators who developed plots for Dick and Jane stories understood their power to influence the behavior of millions of children. At a time when values in America were shifting dramatically, and the number of children in classrooms was growing, Dick and Jane became role models whose words

The Dog for Dick

Father said, "Come with me.
I want to get something for Spot."

"Oh, Father," said Dick.
"We want to look at the dogs now."

45

Jane said, "Look at this little dog!
It wants to play with us."

Sally said, "Jump, little dog.
Jump! Jump! Jump!
We like you."

Dick said, "Down, Spot, down.
I want to see the little dogs."

46

"See that big red boat," said Dick.
"I want a new boat."

"Oh, Dick," said Sally.
"You have a yellow boat."

"Yes," said Jane.
"You have one boat.
Do you want two?"

"I guess not," said Dick.
"I guess I will go home and
play with my yellow boat."

"Good-by, little duck," said Sally.
"I will go home and
play with my yellow duck."

"Good-by, baby doll," said Jane.
"I will go home and
play with my two big dolls."

"Good-by, red boat," said Dick.
"We will all go home and
play with the toys we have."
And they all ran home.

and actions were used to illustrate mainstream values of the time. Family, responsibility, citizenship and the importance of work were foremost. But at a time when children were gaining an upper hand, and adults were fretting over all the choices American culture was throwing their way, kind and considerate Dick and Jane had to come to terms with their own conflicting desires and postwar acquisitiveness. In "Who Wants a Toy?," Dick and Jane and Sally learn to be happy with the toys they already have. In "The Dog for Dick," Dick comes to understand the need for kindness and consideration, even toward animals.

Dick said, "Look here, Father.
This little dog likes us.
And we like it.
Will you get it for us?"

Father said, "You have a dog.
What will you do with Spot?
Do you want Spot to go away?"

Jane said, "Look at Spot!
Spot wants to run away now."

Dick said, "Oh, Spot!
I like that little dog.
But I do not want it.
I want my dog!
I want you!"

Heaven and Health

Parochial schools—a substantial religious educational market—asked Scott Foresman to produce religious editions of their popular textbooks. In 1930 the company obliged, replacing regular Dick and Jane stories with new ones that promoted Catholic values. By the 1950s, Dick and Jane and Sally had been rechristened John and Jean and Judy, named for Catholic saints. Spot, Puff, Mother and Father kept their own names.

In one pre-primer story, "Jesus Is Here," Mother and Father drive the family to church, where Dick and Jane and Sally will pray for Jesus' help. Spot and Puff, who'd like to go to church too, have to stay in the car. In "Blessed Mother Mary and Baby Jesus," Father surprises the family when he brings home a framed picture of the Virgin Mary cuddling the Baby Jesus. The children become excited when he hangs it above a vase of flowers in a place of honor in the living room. In "The Night Baby Jesus Came," John and Father set up a screen and slide projector in the living room and show the story of the Nativity for Jean and an assembled group of her friends. Dick and Jane books were also produced in a Seventh Day Adventist edition.

On another front, Dick and Jane were called into action to teach first-graders about health, personal development and safety. *Good Times with Our Friends* and *Happy Times with Our Friends* appeared in 1948. The Teacher's Edition emphasized that a teacher's first responsibility was to establish the finest physical

Jane said, "Look, look.
It is red.
We can not go now.
Stop, Dick and Sally.
Stop, Spot.
See the cars go.
We do not want to get hurt."

22

The 1941 *Good Times with Our Friends*

environment for her pupils: maintain the classroom at a proper temperature (68°F to 70°F), keep the atmosphere from getting too dry, see that children have properly adjusted chairs and desks, monitor the lighting in the classroom.

Concentrating on health, safety and mental hygiene, stories emphasized: working and playing safely (six-year-olds are accident-prone); the importance of sleep and the willingness to observe a reasonable bedtime hour; an appreciation of milk ("baby food" to most six-year-olds); a willingness to try new foods; proper use of a handkerchief to avoid the spread of germs; as well as good habits in nutrition, dressing, washing and dental care.

The Teacher's Edition reminds teachers that boys and girls should be given "the comforting assurance that they are not alone in their problems or varied emotions, that differences among people are to be prized rather than deplored, that reasonable standards of behavior rather than perfection constitute legitimate goals, that difficult situations usually must be met squarely rather than evaded, and that there are learnable techniques for getting along better with oneself and with others."

These books, like all Dick and Jane books, were not only revised to keep products up-to-date (replacing gauze bandages with band-aids) but also introduced new words to a child's vocabulary: breakfast, wash, milk, hurt, lunch, bump, handkerchief, candy, dinner, clothes, hats, tired, late, clean.

Father said, "Come, come.
Come and find something.
It is for Dick and Jane.
It is for Sally.
Come and find it."

Dick said, "I can find it."
Sally said, "I can find it."

30

The 1941 Cathedral Edition *We Come and Go*

The Power of Positive Thinking

It's an iffy proposition to expect young boys and girls to do the right thing. Someone has to guide them. Parents start the process off, teaching values and drawing moral boundaries. Schools reinforce broader community values and promote social skills. Religious organizations and community and special interest groups also have their say in molding a child's spiritual and civic behavior.

The sense of suburban well-being filled advertisements, dreams and everyday life in the 1950s, but underneath the surface some leftover fears and some new anxieties were eating away at traditional values. Memories of the insecurity and sacrifice of the Depression and World War II gnawed at the belief in upward spiraling progress. The exaggerated threat of encroaching communism and constant atomic anxieties set off by the cold war undermined the sense of safety and security. A 1954 Supreme Court decision barring segregation in public schools exposed widespread racial bias in America. It triggered fears among white Americans who didn't want to share access to the American Dream, while providing some opportunities for blacks. When the Soviets launched Sputnik in 1957 and beat the Americans into space, fingers pointed at educators, who were criticized for not taking math and the sciences seriously.

Separated by geography from families and traditions, people felt stirrings of alienation. A new value system for suburbia mandated conformity, ambition and a frenzied materialism, taking some of the joy out of upward mobility. Mothers and fathers, faced with moral dilemmas and social uncertainty, clung to the hope that by being part of suburbia, they could keep the threatening outside world at bay.

In 1958, the number of people regularly attending churches and synagogues reached its highest level in American history before decline would set in, two years later. Spiritual leader Norman Vincent Peale's book *The Power of Positive Thinking* was a best-seller throughout the decade. It preached that answers to trouble lay within the individual, in the divine energy stored in the unconscious. According to Peale, all a person needed to do was "picturize" a goal, "prayerize" to learn what God wants, and "actualize" positive energy to leave one's troubles behind. By 1957, Peale was reaching a weekly television audience of thirty million believers.

Children were organized into activities that got them out of the house and expanded their repertoire of social skills while reinforcing traditional values. The scouting movement boomed during the 1950s. Brownie and Girl Scout membership rose from 1.8 million to four million. Girl Scouts hustled so many cookies that commercial bakeries had to fill the orders. Cub Scout enrollment doubled from 766,635 in 1949 to 1.6 million in 1956, and across the nation Boy Scouts gave three-fingered salutes as they repeated the Scout Oath: "On my honor, I will do my best: to do my duty to God and my country, and to obey the Scout Law; to help other people at all times; to keep myself physically strong, mentally awake, and morally straight."

On a scouting trip, a Cub Scout, Brownie and Boy Scout paid their respects to the Liberty Bell.

The Perils of
Dick and Jane

Dick and Jane and Sally must have been born under lucky stars. As with all little children, some bad things happen to them. But not too bad. The ball they play with rolls under a car, and only Spot can reach it. Their wagon tips over and Jane tumbles to the ground, but she isn't hurt. Tim falls, over and over again, into a ditch, into the lake, down the stairs, out of the car, but someone always rescues him. When a doll carriage wheel breaks off, Father can repair it. When a dress tears, Mother sits down and mends it.

Wouldn't you know, it's Sally who gets into the most scrapes. She's the baby and makes mistakes because she can't think things through. So because she doesn't pay attention, Sally drops the ice cream from her cone, and lucky Spot and Puff get to lick it up. When Sally offers Tim a drink of water from the fountain in the park, she squirts everybody, and everybody laughs, "Funny, funny Sally." She'll learn. Mother's face powder looks so pretty, Sally has to try some on—on herself, on Tim, then on Puff and, finally, on Spot, who looks doubtful, but only for a moment.

Animals get in trouble too. Puff breaks a balloon, gets trapped in a yarn ball, is stuck up a tree. Spot knocks over Sally's toy farm—two times—and all the little animals topple to the floor! Spot gets chased by angry hens, has a stand-off with a big French poodle and, in his darkest hour, almost runs away when Dick hurts his feelings. A pet rabbit escapes. Little Quack, visiting from a farm, tries to run away too.

But every bit of trouble, which always comes as a surprise in Dick and Jane's world, has a happy ending. Bad things are turned into good things. Dicey moments get resolved without nasty taunts, little fists flying, mean words or tiny tears.

A Shot in the Arm

Outside the charmed world of storybooks, bad things do happen to good little children. Luckily, most of them are minor mishaps. A child loses a favorite toy or breaks something around the house, falls off a bike, gets stung by a bee. A child complains about a tummy ache and parents cope. Children are more vulnerable and need special care when it comes to scarier illnesses like chicken pox, mumps, whooping cough and measles.

It was in the 1950s, after two decades of escalating and frightening epidemics, that the poliomyelitis virus, which attacks nerve cells that control muscle movement, became every parent's nightmare. In 1952, the worst year on record, 58,000 cases of polio were reported and 1,400 children died. Rumor and fear surrounded the contagious illness. Children were kept away from crowded swimming pools, pulled out of movie theaters, and whisked home from summer camps in the middle of the night. In newspapers and newsreels, images of children doomed to death, paralysis or years in an iron lung haunted the fearful nation. Children were terrified at the sight of flies and mosquitoes thought to carry the virus. Parents dreaded fevers and complaints of sore throats or stiff necks.

In 1951, medical researcher Dr. Jonas Salk began testing a vaccine using dead polio viruses powerful enough to trigger antibodies in people who were inoculated with them. By the spring of 1954, the country mobilized to test the vaccine on 650,000 children in forty-four states. Twenty thousand doctors and public health officials, 40,000 nurses, 64,000 schoolteachers and principals and 200,000 volunteers cooperated in running the trials and in analyzing the results. The success of Salk's vaccine made him a hero, ranked in public opinion polls between Winston Churchill and Mahatma Gandhi.

David Eisenhower (*far right*), grandson of President Dwight Eisenhower, lined up for his polio vaccination.

Easy-to-Read Instructions

During World War II, many women left teaching for higher paying factory jobs and to help the wartime effort. When the war ended, with the baby boom swelling school populations, new teachers were hired, but they often had inadequate training.

That's why Teacher's Editions, which had been part of the Scott Foresman system for many years, became so important to the success of the Dick and Jane reading method. Charged with marching armies of children through the educational system, educators developed instructions for teaching reading that were as reliable as the recipes on cake boxes.

The Teacher's Editions explained what a complicated process reading really was and outlined a clear plan of attack that any teacher could follow. The guides also urged teachers to understand that the needs of each child they taught were different. The 1951 Teacher's Edition to the Dick and Jane pre-primers explained: "Children do not leave their problems behind when they come to school.... Not all homes are happy or filled with warmth and understanding of children. There are noisy, crowded homes surrounded by dirt and squalor.... There are homes where standards of order and cleanliness come first and children second. There are broken homes and unhappy homes where the child feels no sense of belonging....

There are homes in which the air is charged with conflict. When such deprived children lose themselves in stories about Dick, Jane, and Sally, and live for a time with these happy storybook characters, they experience the same release from their problems that the adult does when he loses himself in a good book or a movie.... Family conflicts, the absence of a "real" father or mother, the strain of high standards, or the sense of neglect are forgotten...."

Detailed lesson plans showed teachers the path that moved them through every page of the reading program. For less experienced teachers, scripts suggested the exact words to be repeated if they were to do their jobs successfully. Each lesson was organized around four sections: "Preparing for Reading," "Interpreting the Story," "Extending Skills and Abilities" and "Extending Interests." To teach the pre-primer story "Jump and Play," the teacher begins the class with a discussion of games like hopscotch, leapfrog and jump rope to get youngsters talking about their favorite games. Then, using word cards or writing on the blackboard, the teacher presents the two new words in the story, "you" and "not," and uses them in sentences so children recognize the form of the word and the context in which it can be used. Still "preparing," teachers then ask questions to make certain that the children comprehend the examples.

First-graders, like these Cleveland students, spent 40 percent of their school day learning to read.

In the most important section of the lesson, "Interpreting the Story," here's what the Teacher's Edition advises:

Guided reading: *Open the books to the table of contents and see if the youngsters can find the name of today's story. "It's a jump-rope story," you can hint. "Who can find the name for us?" Later, help everyone find the first page of the story.*

Page 33: *Ask pupils what they think of Father's jumping ability. "Do the children look as if they're enjoying this game?" After the silent reading of the text, ask, "To whom was Sally talking? What did she want Mother to see? What did Sally think of Father? Does Father look funny to you, too?" Following the oral reading, return to the picture again and ask, "Whom else do you see in this picture? Did anyone in the story notice Spot and Puff? What do you think Spot and Puff are doing?"*

Page 31: *"Who is in this picture? What are Dick and Jane doing? What do you suppose they plan to do?" Talk about why Dick might be waving and what the two children could be saying. Draw attention to the name of the story and ask someone to read it aloud."*

Page 34: *Guide the detailed interpretation with such questions as: "What has happened? What do you suppose Jane said? Read the first three lines to yourselves. Who can not jump and play? Is Father the only one who can not jump?" Have the group read the rest of the page to themselves to find out what Dick said.*

Page 32: *Girls and boys may be surprised to see Mother joining the game. "Do you think this was fun? What makes you think everyone in the story likes it, too?" Notice Sally's excitement and welcome ideas on what she may have said. Ask someone to read aloud Sally's speech before you call attention to the fact that Dick had another idea. Have pupils read the last three lines silently to find out what it was. "What was Dick's idea?" Continue by having the last three lines read aloud. After the entire page has been read as a unit, ask, "Do you suppose Father can jump rope as well as Mother can? What makes you say so?"*

After the children reread this story, the section "Extending Skills and Abilities" suggests activities to develop memory and phonetic skills and to reinforce the meaning of the two new words. Finally, in "Extending Interests," the teacher reads aloud two poems about hopping and jumping as children clap and jump along, plays a recording of one more poem, then organizes a jumping contest.

On the Town

Wherever town is, it's not far from home. Sometimes Mother walks there. Sally drives alongside in her metal toy car, and Dick and Jane travel the same route in their red wagon. When they arrive, no one is too tired to shop. Sometimes they take the big bus and look through the windows at the changing scene. There are traffic signs to read and stoplights to pay attention to. Town is a busy, clean, pleasant place, a place to learn grown-up things. There's a main street, lined with cheerful big picture windows piled with things boys and girls like to look at. They learn what it means to shop and that everything has its price. They understand they can't have everything.

Dick, Jane, Sally and Mother go to the grocery store often, where they see pyramids of delicious fruit and bins of healthy vegetables and, in the bakery section, stare at the pink frosted cupcakes temptingly set out in neat rows. Sally gets to browse for a new book at the bookstore, spinning a book rack around and around. Jane window-shops for a new doll. Everyone gets new out-fits for holidays and when it's time to head back to school. Because they behave, the kids get ice cream treats at the soda fountain.

When they leave the main street, there's more to see. There's the service station with lights and gas pumps where Father takes the car to have it checked. There's a zoo filled with elephants, hippos and kanga-roos who are fun to look at and even more fun to imitate. But there's no place better than the Fun Park, where there's a merry-go-round that goes up and down and faster and faster and scary rides that make kids squeal with joy. Jane likes the game of ring toss best, because she beats Dick and Father. Atta girl!

Copycats

Dick and Jane books were such successful readers, and baby boomers such a big educational market, that competing textbook pub-lishers came up with copycat versions of the winning Dick and Jane formula. To gain their share of the market, they introduced other brother and sister teams, of which Alice and Jerry (Row, Peterson and Company), Susan and Tom (Ginn and Company), and Ned and Nancy (D.C. Heath and Company) were the most popular. Bill and Susan, Tags and Twinkle, Bill and Linda and Jack and Jane had their followings too.

Alice and Jerry

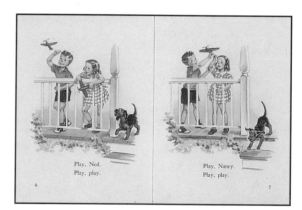

Ned and Nancy

Susan and Tom

Car culture so dramatically changed the American landscape, that a 1965 Highway Beautification Act encouraged communities to plant trees and flowers alongside roads, while the federal government legislated the placement and sizes of roadside signage.

Drive-by Culture

No technological invention has changed the way Americans live as radically as the automobile. From a temperamental plaything, the car became a necessity. The automobile changed the landscape and the way we saw it; it changed how cities were built, and ultimately how we lived.

In 1930, twenty-three million cars were on the road; by 1950 that number had doubled. Eight million cars, the highest number to date, were built in the U.S. in 1955. New car sales totaling $65 billion accounted for 20 percent of America's gross national product. The car was driving the American economy, an optimistic symbol of change and progress. Charles E. Wilson, the former president of General Motors who became President Eisenhower's Secretary of Defense, admitted the obvious: "What was good for our country was good for General Motors, and vice versa."

From 1940 to 1950, the number of highway miles built almost tripled, from 234,000 to 641,000. The practical value of driving on new roads paled in comparison to the other values Americans projected on their cars in the 1950s—to reflect and fantasize about themselves, their status and, most important, their mobility and freedom. Car ownership touched the deepest recesses of the American psyche: You were what you drove. General Motors figured out and targeted markets for each of its products, according to how much consumers would spend and where on the social ladder they saw themselves. Blue-collar workers and young couples just starting out bought Chevys. More confident, successful people who wanted a sportier look chose Pontiacs. Oldsmobiles looked good to white-collar bureaucrats. Buicks were for the local doctor, the lawyer and young professionals on the rise. The Cadillac was the ultimate status symbol for the executive at the top of the ladder.

Americans were ready to trade in newly won stability for mobility, to abandon tradition for a chance to see the "new" world

being built. The Sunday drive to the relatives may have been the first on-the-road ritual, but soon people were driving for the fun of it, making up destinations—to the airport to see new jet planes, to neighborhoods where people with more money lived—or just driving around to see what was new. Sundays were no longer for rest, but for shopping in stores that did one-third of their weekly business on that day. Family vacations in the car were another kind of ritual, a quest for education, relaxation and open spaces that quickly became dotted with billboards and roadside attractions meant to lure people off the highways. Architecture and signage, scaled to the motorist's viewpoint, created a roadside environment designed to make an impact at high speed.

The car changed how Americans shopped, as Main Street lost its monopoly, its customers and its luster. Shiny, modern franchises—McDonald's, AAMCO, Holiday Inn, Roto-Rooter, H & R Block, Kentucky Fried Chicken, Dunkin' Donuts, Midas Muffler, Cut & Curl—opened across the country. Each sold an imaginative concept and a predictable product. Advertised locally and nationally, franchises hastened the death of many mom-and-pop businesses, which by comparison seemed slow, shoddy, expensive and old-fashioned. A growing nation on the go wanted speed, efficiency, predictable products and a smiley but impersonal "Hello" and "Thank you," before they jumped back in the car.

Baby boomers were the first generation to be driven before they walked. Cars changed parents' relationships with their teenagers, who, as soon as they were old enough, grabbed for car keys, expressing their independence and looking for entertainment. Cars became couches, where couples found privacy. And by the early 1960s, the car had even become a place to pray when the first drive-in church opened in California; worshipers sat in their "pews from Detroit" and heard sermons broadcast over loudspeakers.

On the Road

In this one-car family, Father drives. Mother sits up front next to Father, and the children and Spot, and sometimes even Puff and Tim, sit in the back. The big four-door sedan is Father's special appliance, and he washes and simonizes it to keep it looking new. Father loves his car. He knows exactly what the motor sounds like. If it doesn't purr like Puff, if it clinks, or clicks, or rattles, off it goes to the service station. Sometimes it just needs gas. Dick and Jane love to go along to watch, to see the numbers spin as the gas tank fills. They like the funny smell of gasoline. And they watch with fascination as attendants—in bow ties, neat uniforms and smart caps—put on a show. Open the hood. Check the oil. Add water to the radiator. Wash the windshield. Check the tires. Take the money. And when Father starts the car, they wave a friendly good-bye.

On the road, the air feels cool on Dick and Jane's faces. The wind rushes through Sally's curly hair. The car smells like metal, like rubber, like wool. It's fun to sit on the deep car seat, legs dangling above the floor. The car is a beautiful thing, with carpeting, molded plastic locks, stitched upholstery, leather piping, armrests and shiny chrome ashtrays. It's fun to look out the car windows and see trees and buildings and people and other cars go by so fast, to see small things far away get so big, to see big things get so small.

Every time they climb in the family car,

which is almost as big as a room in their house, Dick and Jane and Sally have something to look forward to. A car ride is a treat, not something that happens every day. The car is for drives to special places—not to school or the grocery store—but to the new model houses, to Grandmother and Grandfather's farm, to the lake for a boat ride or a picnic, to the zoo and, once in a while, to the Fun Park.

The family's first car was big and green. Then every five years or so Father got a new one. A sportier car. Then a station wagon. That's how time and progress are measured in Dick and Jane's world, and it's not just the cars that change, but who's in the driver's seat. By 1962, Mother's behind the wheel, and Dick and Jane and Sally can't imagine a day without the fun of a drive.

85

What You See Is What You Get

Before baby boomers were old enough to read words with Dick and Jane, they were already experts in "reading" pictures. They were growing up in a visual culture where comics, movies, magazines, billboards, store signs, mall order catalogs and, most of all, television showed them—rather than told them—about a world that was vivid, seductive and constantly changing.

Changes in American culture could be measured visually. The exciting ways things could look, the way styles appeared virtually overnight, redefined America as a modern, prosperous, imaginative country. The golden age of consumer culture offered up one new experience, then replaced it with another option. With so many new objects and events swirling around them, people could take pleasure just in looking. Adults and children were excited window-shoppers, surveying new homes and furnishings, clothes and foodstuffs, toys and gadgets before they made their choices. Just seeing so many objects change shape—cars, appliances, hairdos— gave people a sense that the shape of their own lives could change too, and get better and better and better.

After two decades of seeing black-and-white images of a drab, deprived world, the fifties introduced colored cereals, colored appliances and colorful magazine advertisements that promoted optimism and progress to adults and children. Jingle-driven television commercials grabbed kids' attention as they stared at ads for everything, making up their own minds about what was good, what was bad, what was necessary, and what they wanted their own worlds to look like.

Kids already knew what other tiny worlds looked like in pictures. Comic books, popular since the 1930s, taught kids how to "read" stories one frame at a time by studying drawings of characters' gestures, expressions and costumes. They became versatile in decoding comic book graphic shorthand—people "saw" stars when they were punched, light bulbs lit up over characters' heads when they had an idea, something moving across a scene left a trail of black lines.

Adults had their picture books too. Magazines arrived weekly—*Life*, *Look*, *The Saturday Evening Post*. Everything was described in picture stories that even kids could figure out: how the president of France spent the day, what a movie star ate for breakfast, what an atom bomb looked like as it exploded. Children could even learn things they weren't supposed to by scrutinizing half-naked bodies in *National Geographic* or the underwear pages of the Sears catalog.

In 1953, a billion comic books were sold at a cost of four times the U.S. library book budget.

Just as interesting as the picture stories were the sophisticated, colorful advertisements that used visual tricks to make chicken pot pies or new convertibles look like they were jumping off the page.

Kids also took their own pictures and using black photo corners glued them into story sequences in family photo albums. Kids were the child stars of home movies, parading back and forth, making faces, always waving, gesturing and mouthing words at the camera. View-Master slide sets supplied 3-D escape routes, and once a week there were the movies, bigger than life.

At the movies was where kids made their strongest, most visceral connection to pictures. Kids used their imaginations to project themselves into the pictures on a screen, to get lost in history or in a science fiction nightmare, to chase the bad guys over a mountain. Sitting in the dark, in the first row or in the back of the balcony, kids added to their repertoire of visual know-how, catching on to how to react to close-ups, long shots, fade-ins and fade-outs and grasping how movies create their own sense of time and reality.

But it was television that finally defined this first visually literate generation as separate from their parents. In the mid-1950s, six-year-olds who were just getting their first Dick and Jane reading readiness book had already watched 5,000 hours of TV programs. By the time they reached sixth grade, they averaged four and a half hours of TV viewing daily, and more than six hours on Sunday. Watching television began to take up one-quarter of a child's life.

Short shows and even shorter commercials trained kids to expect and be ready to switch gears, to jump from an engrossing story to a seductive commercial, to another commercial, to station identification, and then back into the story without missing a narrative beat. Television delivered more information in a day than a teacher could teach in a week. Changing collages of images defined a new reality, linking kids together through the shows they watched and loved.

The visual world was providing its own curriculum. Children learned more of what they needed to know from the pictures they saw—at home, on the street, at the supermarket, in magazines, on television and in movie theaters. This was the first generation to know the world through pictures first—to depend on, and even to value, fast, sophisticated and entertaining pictures more than words.

We Look and See

From the 1946 Pre-primer Teacher's Edition

When people remember Dick and Jane, what pops to mind first are the simple words they learned to read. "Look," "See," "Jump," "Oh," "Run." What is less obvious is how great a role the illustrations had in developing skills children had to master before they could read.

William Gray and his cohorts at Scott Foresman were ahead of their time in understanding how important pictures had become in a modern world that was relying more and more on visual information. In a 1946-47 Teacher's Edition, Gray wrote: "Skill in interpreting pictures is becoming increasingly important as a means of securing pleasure and information. Adults today are exposed to 'picture' magazines, cartoons, advertisements, movies, and many types of diagrammatic schemes for the presentation of facts. Children are surrounded with picture books and 'read' the funnies long before they enter school. Regardless of age or situation, the individual who can 'read' pictorial material effectively has access to a vast world of new ideas."

Illustrations in Dick and Jane books worked just as hard as the words printed beneath them. It was the pictures, full of drama and surprise, that really told the stories. As simple as they might seem, they were complex, full of details and information that a child could study and discover: the kind of sneakers Dick wore, how a sprinkler attached to a hose, how Mother bent her knees when she jumped rope. Movie-like, they looked spontaneous and true-to-life because the illustrators worked from photographs.

The teachers encouraged each student to tell a story based upon what he or she had seen in the picture, making certain that the most important incidents were noted. The next step was to introduce a group of pictures that told a story, so students learned to interpret the narrative in a picture sequence. These sequences were called "talking-picture stories."

Students were trained to look carefully at an individual picture, and did exercises in their workbooks identifying the details of what they saw. For instance, a teacher would say, "This picture shows many things happening at one time. Look at it carefully. What do you see?" Teachers encouraged their classes to make inferences about things a picture implied. "What season is it? Is it late spring or summer?" By leading children to notice the clothing worn, the leaves on the tree, the presence of a robin, teachers helped them understand what was implied by a picture, the information that wasn't spelled out but could be figured out. And by studying the differences among objects in a row and figuring out which were alike and which were different, children learned skills they needed to discriminate between one letter form and the next.

In show-and-tell sessions, children brought snapshots or pictures from newspapers and magazines that related to the stories they studied. The pictures were thumbtacked to bulletin boards or arranged in stories in a scrapbook. With so much time spent "reading" the information in pictures, it's not surprising that postwar children were well prepared to navigate a world that, as time passed, was packed with more and more visual information that moved or changed, faster and faster.

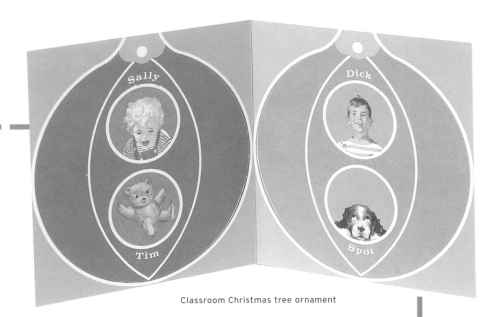

Classroom Christmas tree ornament

Love, from Dick and Jane

At the peak of their popularity in the 1950s, Dick and Jane controlled 80 percent of the early reading market. First-graders loved them so much that they sent Dick and Jane thousands of letters a year, most of them asking whether or not the children had a last name. And, as polite, thoughtful children would do, Dick and Jane wrote back. Year after year, teachers and students got Valentines, Christmas cards that could be hung on classroom trees, as well as calendars, pens, pencils and even party napkins.

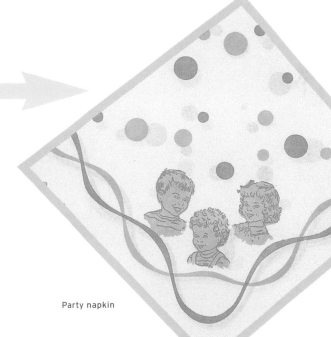

Party napkin

Valentine's Day card

89

3. Growing Up wi

th Dick and Jane

At the brink of adulthood, young people in the 1960s looked out over a vista of change, accelerating in every direction. Against a kaleidoscopic backdrop of fun—acid rock, pop art, fast-paced movies, psychedelic posters and outrageous fashions—the media broadcast starker pictures of political and social conflicts, at home and abroad. Teenagers never knew what they were going to see or hear: Laugh-In or another assassination, *Love Story* or *Easy Rider*, Connie Francis or Janis Joplin. It was time to make choices, time to test the limits and, for some, time to rebel.

Raised during a prolonged period of world peace, baby boomers were the most educated, sophisticated and mobile generation the country had turned out. Blessed with a sense of economic security unmatched in history, many were uncomfortable being so comfortable, and were ready to blast off—to be outrageous instead of polite, to reject repression and "let it all hang out."

The cold war had escalated into a deadly political power game. When the young, handsome President John F. Kennedy faced down Nikita Khrushchev over the stockpiling of Soviet missiles in Cuba, tearful baby boomers, watching TV, got their first terrifying whiff of mortality. Nothing, not even security, could be taken for granted. It was obvious, when they read the daily news and looked out their car windows, that while the suburbs might be affluent, cities had become unmanageable, and parts of them unlivable. The gap between privilege and poverty had never been so wide, so clear. A war in Southeast Asia was beginning to cast its dark shadow.

In his inaugural address, the charismatic Kennedy had challenged American youth to take action: "... ask not what your country can do for you; ask what you can do for your country." Many responded to his idealism by looking around to see where they might make a difference. With no allegiance to the past, and numbers on their side, they would shake up the country.

1960

Student demonstrations, peaceful in the early sixties, became increasingly violent as the decade progressed. In 1964, Berkeley police dragged away protesters who had turned university property into a "People's Park."

The youngest President ever elected, John F. Kennedy projected an image of energy and intellect, family and fun. His moving speeches motivated young Americans to join the Peace Corps and embrace their responsibility as citizens.

By the mid-1960s, high school enrollment had doubled from the previous decade. Twenty million eighteen-to-twenty-four-year-olds were ready to leave home. Some went to college. Some moved south to register black voters. Others went overseas and down the economic ladder, to join the Peace Corps to build schools, health centers and housing for people who could give only their thanks in return.

But in 1963, bullets brought down Kennedy and his vision and shattered the American Dream. Violence slammed shut the gate on the New Frontier, and created a void that some distraught young people had the courage to look into. Everyone was stunned by the country's loss. Some people couldn't move forward and others felt they had nothing left to lose. They rejected the repressive codes of the 1950s, and exposed the hypocrisy of the world they were heirs to. With a precocity and surprising assurance gleaned from the media that had nourished them, they would change the world by triggering a decade of skepticism, rebellion, radical experimentation and instability.

While Dick and Jane were teaching yet another generation of first-graders to "help" and "work" and have "fun," articulate former first-graders were screaming, "Up the establishment," "Tell it like it is" and, above all, "Don't trust anyone over thirty." The rules and values drummed into their heads by parents who had lived through the Depression and a world war did not make any sense in a world where "do your own thing" was replacing family "togetherness" as the rallying cry for a generation. Kennedy had promised a New Frontier, and now Lyndon Johnson was hell-bent on giving all Americans access to his Great Society.

It would not be so simple. Nuclear families were breaking apart. People were tired of telling lies—about who they were, about who they loved, about why they worked so hard, about whether they were happy. There was a bad fit between traditional norms and new social realities. Between a quarter and a third of the people who married in the 1950s were on the road to divorce. The generation

When the single "She Loves You" was released in 1963, Beatlemania hit America. Flower power peaked in 1968, and the Beatles' animated cartoon, *Yellow Submarine*, dazzled audiences with psychedelic animation and clever lyrics.

Under the leadership of Martin Luther King, Jr., southern blacks organized nonviolent marches to register the eleven million blacks who through poll taxes and trumped-up literacy tests had been deprived of their right to vote. The road from Selma to Montgomery, Alabama in 1965 had to be placed under National Guard protection.

It was a time to test the limits. Young people

gap widened when young people refused to turn into Mother or Father. Who needed to listen to parents when there was an edgier counterculture to live in as well as millions of peers who agreed it was time to be different?

When the largest freshman class ever hit college in 1963, their demands for change couldn't be silenced by nervous school administrators. Students held rap sessions, teach-ins, sit-ins, and called strikes to topple values that had stood for generations. Students at Berkeley, many back from civil rights demonstrations in the South, returned with new organizational skills. The Free Speech Movement began when they protested the university's ban on fund-raising and recruiting for political causes on campus. Their action crystallized a national political movement around the New Left.

Middle-class students, sensing that political action would be cleansing, began to identify with the oppressed. They did it out of guilt, for the romance of being involved, as an apprenticeship. Their support would jump from one social cause to another, because they now understood that progress was not automatic. A domino principle was at work. Sparks from the civil rights movement inflamed students who insisted that there was no part of America that couldn't be improved. The women's movement shook up America's psyche, with women demanding equal rights in the kitchen, the bedroom and the boardroom. A sexual revolution was in the works. People either postponed getting married, or didn't bother to marry at all. The birth rate dropped by a third. This was the first generation that made having a child a life-style choice. Gay liberation gave voice to men and women who no longer had to hide who they loved. Consumer rights activists pointed fingers at corporations that built unsafe cars and perfected napalm. The economic growth that everyone had cheered and hoped to share in now was a threat to the whole earth and its fragile environment. And the urban black population, which had doubled since the 1950s, had won its civil rights but now had to battle for fair treatment.

By the mid-1960s, former Dicks and Janes, well-behaved children who had stayed within the lines in their coloring books,

The U.S. started bombing Vietnam in 1965. By 1967, the first major antiwar marches, in New York and Washington, D.C., were covered worldwide by the media, and in the first six months of 1968, 221 demonstrations rocked college campuses. While 58,196 Americans died, hawks and doves debated the morality of America's involvement, until the war ended in 1973.

At Woodstock, the landmark "Aquarian Exposition" held on a dairy farm in upstate New York in the summer of 1969, 400,000 people braved heat, traffic jams, rain and mud for peace, love and sixty hours of rock and blues.

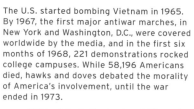

looked out over a vista of change, and with assura

found their fun by acting out. Tie-dyed psychedelic T-shirts were more fun than button-down shirts. Men wore bracelets, women wore more bracelets, and everyone wore love beads. Dogs like Spot wore bandannas. People didn't get dressed, they "dressed up" as sherpas, gypsies, swamis, in costumes of see-through gauze, leather, velvet, showing off their bodies and their individuality. People searched for gurus to help them understand who they were, not what they were supposed to be. Self-expression no longer meant buying a new car every two years, but smoking marijuana and dropping acid. By 1967, "The Summer of Love," these long-haired flower children defined a movement whose social, stylistic and spiritual fallout turned America upside down.

Angrily and visibly, American students opposed the country's involvement in Vietnam and hastened its end. By 1968, the government was spending $30 billion a year on an increasingly unpopular war that many people thought was immoral. Protest turned into resistance. Citizens refused to pay income taxes, burned draft cards and flags and moved to Canada or Sweden to avoid serving in the Army. It was a

turning point in American history. Never had a population turned a war's course through widespread civil protest. America's failure to win the war proved that the country's military power could not be used to justify influencing the politics of another country. America's confident sense of itself as the world's democratic role model and policeman— responsibilities assumed after World War II ended—was shattered by the debacle of Vietnam.

The late 1960s were starting to look like the flip side of the 1940s. Fathers had wanted to fight in a just cause; sons were refusing to fight in a "dirty" war. Mothers who had devoted their lives to homemaking couldn't understand why their daughters weren't settling down. Parents who had sacrificed their personal freedom to keep the bonds of nuclear families intact watched their children disdain family values.

At the schoolhouse too, revolution was underway. Students were changing. Elementary kids started school wiser than students before them. They may have cut their teeth watching *Romper Room* and *Ding Dong School* on TV, but

Sixties technologies turned science fiction into reality. Scientists decoded DNA molecules and generated laser light waves, while computers navigated astronauts through their landing on the moon on July 20, 1969.

Oral contraception came into widespread use in America by 1960, reflecting the changes in America's attitudes about sexual freedom. Using "the Pill," American women could choose to protect themselves against unwanted pregnancies for the first time. By the end of the decade, 80 percent of college men and women surveyed said premarital sex was just fine.

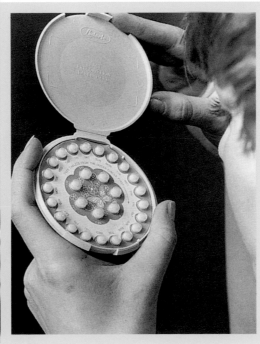

nce they changed the world by triggering a decade

they came of age stunned by the evening news, full of war and violence. When student demonstrators at the 1968 Democratic National Convention screamed, "The whole world's watching," as they were beaten by Chicago cops, children were watching too. Kids were wrenched from their storybook lives. Those who lived in one-parent homes took care of themselves when no one else was around. Kids were sophisticated and street-wise, privy to secrets children had been shielded from before—offensive language, sex, racial hatred, and the out-of-control quality of everyday life. The barriers that protected childhood were gone.

Children's experiences in schools were changing too. Kids were being bused out of their own neighborhoods into unfamiliar schools in strange territories. In urban and suburban schools, geographic and racial universes apart, parents and teachers called for books that showed more than a white middle-class suburban world. Forward-thinking elementary school educators, working in university think tanks, were determined to find a way of presenting a more complex world to media-savvy, street-smart kids.

As American institutions were shaken to their core, so was the world of Dick and Jane. From the start, the stories—text, illustration and content—had been adapted and revised taking into account the changing world of the readers. Characters and situations shed their traditional look and were modernized. The easy part was updating illustrations of the clothes, the house and the family car. Mother learned to drive, Father learned to cook, and Dick and Jane and Sally, from time to time, were now less than perfect.

Changing the cast of characters, so that Dick and Jane's world was more diverse, was harder. New people moved into the neighborhood who didn't look anything like Dick and Jane. In 1965, Mike and Pam and Penny and their parents were the first black family on the block and the first to appear in a first-grade basal reading program. Educational publishing was growing up, and so were Dick and Jane.

Across the country, young people in the late 1960s gathered at love-ins to smoke marijuana, renounce capitalism and spread the doctrine of peace and love. Of the 30,000 Flower Children, Love Children and Free People, 70 percent came from middle-class families.

of experimentation.

The New Neighbors

They're here! Mike and the cute little twins, Pam and Penny. Their pretty Mother and handsome Father are here too. It's 1965, and they're the new neighbors who live next door or maybe just down the block. They make great new friends for Dick and Jane and Sally. And like Dick and Jane and Sally's family, they don't have a last name either. Mike and Pam and Penny like to have fun and to work too. And they are happy.

Mike is just like Dick. He's the same height, wears the same kind of clothes and runs around just as much. Mike's a leader too. He is Dick's first real friend, and more than his match at games, bike-riding and making up new things to do. Mike is great at guessing games. He organizes puppet shows, makes chalk drawings on Dick's driveway and puts on a play that makes everyone laugh. Mike's a gentleman too, neat and well-

behaved. Just as Dick and Jane watch out for Sally, Mike watches out for Pam and Penny, even though they are good at taking care of each other.

Pam and Penny are identical twins, exactly alike, adorable with their braided pigtails tied in bows or clipped with colorful barrettes. Sometimes they wear overalls, with matching pink tops with their names, so no one gets them confused. Pam and Penny are as lively and mischievous as Sally and twice as much to handle. They're curious. They climb where they shouldn't. Count on the twins to discover the pink cupcakes before the picnic even starts.

The new kids on the block have the best two-wheeler and tricycles. Mike threads colorful strips of plastic through the wheels and from the ends of the handlebars so they fly in the wind when the kids pedal fast. Mike has big books and Pam and Penny have little books. Mike and the twins read a lot. And they work hard in the yard, helping Father, and in the kitchen, helping Mother. Father drives the car and does a lot of gardening, mowing the lawn and trimming shrubs. Mother cooks and helps outside too. She loves to plant red geraniums.

Mike and Pam and Penny live in a house like Dick and Jane's, except it is made of beautiful stones like the path that leads to their front door. From inside their house, you can see outside through the big picture window. Their living room is as comfortable as Dick and Jane's, but they have landscape paintings on the walls and a couch and chairs you want to sink into. Their Mother's shiny kitchen has modern Formica countertops. The new neighbors have style.

Mike and Pam and Penny have Grandparents too. Their Grandmother and Grandfather live in the city in a brownstone apartment house. When the kids visit, they travel by bus, take taxis and go for interesting walks along busy streets. They see all  kinds of city things like big construction sites with thick steel girders, a big old red brick school, streets lined with parking meters and filled with cars. Lucky kids. They get to see things that Dick and Jane and Sally only see on television.

Black in a White World

Dick and Jane's world was populated by white people, and white people only, until the 1960s. Designed to sell all across the country, Dick and Jane books reflected what mainstream educators believed America believed in and did not take into account, because no argument was made for, questions of cultural diversity and alternate points of view.

Black children in the South, where the law mandated separation, attended segregated, underfunded elementary schools where, more often than not, they got an inferior education. They spent the day in dilapidated buildings and were taught by untrained teachers, hampered by out-of-date teaching materials and limited supplies. In the 1950s, educator and psychologist Kenneth B. Clark described how segregating black children in schools lowered their motivation and contributed to negative self-images. Clark said that since children weren't encouraged to aspire to success, they saw no point in trying to excel at schoolwork.

It took the ground-breaking 1954 Supreme Court ruling *Brown* v. *Board of Education of Topeka* to shake up the segregated school systems that Americans took for granted. The court ruled unanimously that "separate but equal" was unconstitutional and institutional segregation therefore could not be tolerated. But desegregation went slowly at first in the South, where school boards often chose to shut down rather than face integration, and later in the North, where white flight to the suburbs insured de facto separation of the races in inner city schools.

Mass migrations of blacks out of the South accelerated in the 1950s and 1960s, as people uprooted their lives and moved to northern cities seeking greater opportunities in jobs and education. They moved in just as whites were moving out to suburbia. Between 1950 and 1960, the black urban population doubled, as 70 percent of the nation's blacks settled in the country's largest cities. Instead of life improving for many, it got worse. Unable to find decent jobs, they felt mounting frustration as they faced continued racial bigotry and economic stagnation.

The civil rights movement gained momentum during the 1960s, as blacks raised consciousness and challenged laws, often through nonviolent demonstrations and civil disobedience. They registered voters, sat in at whites-only lunch counters and held strikes to protest unfair treatment of blacks. The movement's efforts culmi-

At the 1963 March on Washington, 250,000 people supporting pending civil rights bills heard Martin Luther King, Jr. speak about his hopes for the future: "I have a dream that one day... little black boys and black girls will be able to join hands with little white boys and white girls and walk together as sisters and brothers."

nated when the 1964 Civil Rights Act created sweeping guidelines for the preservation of civil liberties, from voting rights to the withholding of federal funds from schools that practiced discrimination.

By the mid-1960s, popular culture started to make room for black entertainers, who had been influencing American culture since the turn of the century, without getting much credit for it. Market and the power of the pocketbook were the path to acceptance. Motown Records, for example, could top the charts because blacks *and* whites could follow its beat, feel its soul, and buy its records. On TV, black performers like Bill Cosby in *I Spy* (1965) and Diahann Carrol, who starred in *Julia* (1968), were successful because they could fit a white mold and disprove racist typecasting at the same time.

Despite gains, the battle for equality raged on among those urban blacks who faced relentless poverty and day-to-day racism. In the second half of the 1960s, anger and frustration spread, fueled by the murders of civil rights leaders Medgar Evers in 1963, black nationalist Malcolm X in 1965 and the Rev. Martin Luther King, Jr., in 1968. Riots broke out in Cleveland, Detroit, Newark, Oakland and New York. In 1965, as the Watts area in Los Angeles went up in flames, four thousand people were injured and thirty-four killed. And during the first nine months of 1967, there were 164 race-based disorders in 128 American cities. The 1968 Kerner Commission report on urban violence concluded: "Our Nation is moving toward two societies, one black, one white—separate and unequal."

Out of the indifference and pain, blacks reassessed their own identity and celebrated their own power. Black became beautiful. The black power movement grew. By end of the sixties, two-thirds of eligible black voters had been registered and 1,200 black candidates had been elected to political office. Black entrepreneurs began to replace white absentee landlords in local businesses. College students participated in strikes, sit-ins and lock-outs, demanding that black studies programs be added to university curricula.

On the elementary school level, these social changes and challenges were felt just as strongly. Empowerment meant that black parents and concerned educators—black and white—would have to redefine what was taught to the youngest of children as they first entered school.

N-O Spells "No"

Dick and Jane were once almost too good to be true. But by the 1960s, like many other Americans, they were changing. Starting in the 1962 editions of Dick and Jane books, the kids looked bigger and older and were more sophisticated. They spent time doing things that were decidedly more cool, like playing basketball and watching TV. Dick and Jane and Sally didn't give up on fun. Their fun was different. They helped Father unpack and set up the new charcoal grill in the backyard. It became their job to feed Spot and Puff. And they used their imaginations in ways they never did before, like when they stared at their shadows and saw Jane as a princess, Dick as a football player and Mike as an Indian chief. And Jane delighted in discovering she had some real power over men, after all. When she trounced Father and Dick in a game of ring toss, she put her hands on her hips, adopting Dick's confident attitude, and laughed at the guys.

The universe that Dick and Jane lived in got bigger. More stylish suburban houses were built, and they filled with new friends. The kids dressed up in plastic space helmets instead of Mother or Father's oversize clothes. The children all knew that the air around them was filled not just with butterflies, but with TV antennas. The sky in suburbia pulsed with television signals. Mother, Dick, Jane and Sally, even Spot and Puff had their favorite TV programs. Fists and voices were raised and an argument broke out when the little kids, Sally or Pam and Penny, blocked the television screen.

What was clear was that Dick and Jane and their crew were more independent and worldly. The kids went off on more far-flung adventures, all on their own. They no longer needed Mother to escort them to the toy store when it was time to buy a birthday present for their friend, little Billy. Dick and Jane shopped on their own, wandering from display to display, looking at shrink-wrapped toys, before they made their decision.

Attitudes changed. Dick and Jane and Sally said words they never would have thought of saying before like, "Help." "Don't." " Can't." "I don't want to." "Get away." "Not now." "No!" They whined a bit and pawned off jobs on each other when they didn't want to do this chore or that. Dick and Jane and Baby Sally had their own priorities. They were full of cute wisecracks when they'd proved themselves right at someone else's expense. And they even pointed fingers and blamed people when they suspected wrongdoing.

And when the fun stopped it was for different reasons than ever before. Father drove his big car over Sally's little toy horse and crushed it in half. He didn't mean to, but Sally was really miserable. To take her mind off her tragedy, to keep her quiet, the whole family piled into the car and drove off to the Fun Park, where they all went off in different directions, seeking their own fun. Sally, too frightened to ride the real white pony (something she liked to do in earlier Dick and Jane books), settled for a spin on the merry-go-round. In the 1950s, when a scoop of ice cream fell off a cone, it was overexcited Spot, jumping up on Sally, who knocked it off. In the 1960s, when ice cream flew, it was because Dick used his pal Tom as a target, dumping his scoop on his friend's head, as a joke.

It was clear that everyone, everything and every place was changing. Even the farm was no longer a safe place. Rabbits now startled ponies who ran away. Plots thickened, and the stories could be almost scary. When Mike disappeared, dogs found his coat in the woods. While everyone was concerned about Mike, something even more dramatic happened. A fire broke out and threatened to burn down the farm. What would happen next?

103

We Watch and Learn

A lot of the world as seen on TV in the 1960s looked nothing like the innocent world long championed in Dick and Jane readers, where childhood was ideal and the emotional soundtrack played songs of unconditional love. Television, now in 95 percent of American homes, brought a constant stream of information—some of it good, some of it bad, and, many critics would say, a lot of it destructive to children. When kids started watching television it changed childhood, because parents and teachers no longer controlled the information kids had access to. Any child could turn a TV set on anytime and *see* what was happening. Innocence gave way to sophistication, while self-sufficiency gave way to a need for constant excitement. The more television kids watched, the harder it became to feel at home in the world of Dick and Jane.

Learning to read was still a thrill. Instead of just sitting and being read to, kids could read for themselves. It was fun to follow the beginning, middle and surprising end of a simple Dick and Jane adventure. But it was easier and more exciting for children to watch TV. Television told stories by piecing together a convincing collage of rapid shots, which kids learned to "read" without any training. By contrast, Dick and Jane's little world seemed unrealistic and tame.

Skills that made kids media-savvy were not the skills they needed to be good readers. As critics have pointed out, the word c-a-t is a symbol that triggers thoughts about the furry, four-legged animal who likes milk, chases mice, and who purrs like Puff when you pet it. When children read the word "cat," their imaginations take off. When they see a cat on TV, they don't have to do any work—it's the specific cat on the TV screen, no imagination required. Another skill that reading demands and TV dulls is the ability to follow a sequence of ideas. When you read, you concentrate on recognizing sequences of letters and words and sentences and paragraphs, which all add up to an idea. When you watch television, so many things happen so fast, there's just enough time to recognize what you see, watch it move and register what you feel. Words are slow, pictures are fast. Words are ideas, pictures are things. Words make us think, pictures make us feel.

Television alone can't be blamed for drops in reading scores, but the more kids watched TV, the more nervous educators got. Some damned the medium as having a bad effect on kids' educational success. Others embraced television as a new tool for teaching. It was smart and inevitable that a maverick group of educational researchers, advertising personnel and producers would harness television to teach disadvantaged kids pre-reading skills on public television, before commercial television lulled and dulled them. Children's Television Workshop's *Sesame Street* debuted in the summer of 1969. It was an innovative program that wound up appealing to all kids. *Sesame Street*, set in an old neighborhood on an inner city street, used short commercial-length spots to capture viewers' attention. Each show was comprised of thirty to fifty separate segments, some as short as twelve seconds. Shows populated by Jim Henson's puppets, real people and cartoon characters taught numbers and letters at first, then went on to tackle social, ethical, environmental and racial issues. Kids who watched the show shared a little world with characters like Big Bird, a seven-foot-tall canary, Oscar the Grouch, Bert, Ernie and the Cookie Monster, a world that was multiethnic and multiracial.

Educational television took a giant step when *Sesame Street* premiered in 1969. Set on a block of an inner-city street, with a multiracial cast, the program broke with educational tradition by exploiting TV techniques to teach skills to preschoolers.

Whatever Happened to Dick and Jane?

Reading theory changes, but the changes come slowly. Once school boards define standards and select the textbooks that will be used, they make a commitment of millions of dollars to a way of teaching and a reading program is firmly set in place. It takes something provocative to rock the establishment, like Rudolf Flesch's book *Why Johnny Can't Read*, which hit the best-seller list in 1955. Flesch claimed that no country had as much trouble teaching reading as America, and blamed the whole word method for making reading English as difficult for kids as Chinese, where every word has its own distinct form. Flesch had a political agenda—the familiar call for a return to America's greatness—and he advocated a return to phonics as a basic step to educational superiority.

From their introduction, Dick and Jane readers were never immune from criticism. Though millions of children were successfully taught to read through Dick and Jane books, some educators complained about the stilted way the characters spoke, about their repetitious language, about their goody-goody behavior. During the 1960s, as American culture was churning, Dick and Jane were challenged on yet another front. Their stories had been based on a family structure that existed in the 1920s—a father, a mother, two or more children. The mother kept house and the father worked.

Pressure groups wanted textbook publishers to show a mother going to work, and a father who did his fair share of housework and child care. Editors were told by teachers and school administrators that the characters had become stereotypes, not right for the time, not representative of the changing demographics of America, its ethnic and racial mix. Special interest groups launched campaigns through local school boards, protesting that society was too complicated for there to be one all-American boy like Dick and one all-American girl like Jane. The books, which had always been adaptable to their milieu, had come to a point where adaptation was really not the answer. Not only Dick and Jane, but the pedagogy that inspired them needed to be rethought, based on the most current information and research about reading.

How to represent multiculturalism in school textbooks had become a core issue, discussed within publishing companies and analyzed in university think tanks. Research groups developed new reading

First-graders, in the late 1940s, reading *We Come and Go*

programs for the large segments of population whose lives and experiences were not being represented in elementary readers. One popular concept was "primacy of speech," an idea that led to introducing street language and, inevitably, street values and diversity into first grade reading materials. Federal funds supported university research to develop appropriate reading programs. In cities like Detroit, Chicago and Pittsburgh, multicultural programs were narrowly adopted, and by the end of the decade had helped to alter mainstream educational publishing.

Dick and Jane had been successful because the reading program worked, and they had represented the American Dream understood by the white, middle-class mainstream. But Dick and Jane were now no longer like the majority of kids who were reading about them, not even white middle-class kids. There was no way Dick and Jane could be believable as the characters they were, saying the words they said and living the lives they lived. It was time for Dick and Jane to retire. And they did, quietly. Scott Foresman continued to sell the 1965 editions of the Dick and Jane books through 1970, when they introduced an entirely new reading system. Today's educational reading programs have leapfrogged over the "real/pretend" world of primers and incorporate actual children's book texts. Children learn to read in a variety of ways and settings, in and out of school, with the teacher, and on their own.

Dick and Jane. Gone, but not forgotten. Say their names and watch a former first-grader's eyes light up. Dick and Jane were introduced as new friends, grew to be trusted role models and were then elevated to American icons. What they represent inspires people. Writers, artists and filmmakers celebrate the brother and sister team. Hip advertisements echo their words. Scholars analyze their pivotal role in American education. Museum exhibitions and television shows keep their history alive.

Dick and Jane reached their peak when America, fresh from winning a war, was secure, safe and flourishing in a burst of prosperity and optimism. Dick and Jane stir memories that have lingered for decades because they remind us of our own histories, especially what it was like to grow up when childhood felt like one long summer day.

Producers/Writers: Carole Kismaric and Marvin Heiferman

Design: Spot Design, New York

Project Manager: Alanna Stang

Text Researchers: Susan Jonas and Marilyn Nissenson

Copy Editor: Paula Glatzer

Interns: Carmen Menocal and Amelia Vicini

Acknowledgments

Collins Publishers San Francisco gratefully acknowledges the creative effort and enthusiasm that Carole Kismaric and Marvin Heiferman, of Lookout, brought to this project, and the guidance and cooperation of Scott, Foresman and Company, especially James M. Fitzmaurice, vice president and editor in chief.

Lookout thanks Jenny Barry, vice president and publisher; Maura Carey Damacion, executive editor; Lynne Noone, production director; and Carole Vandermeyde, executive assistant of Collins Publishers San Francisco, who worked with us to capture the spirit of Dick and Jane. Past and present employees at Scott Foresman who were generous in providing us with materials and information about the history of Dick and Jane readers include: James Fitzmaurice; Nancie Mitchell, associate librarian; Judy Besterfeldt, manager, library and information services; Sandra Belton, executive editor, educational technology; Bert Crossland, product manager, reading; Beth Martin, director of advertising; Judy Nyberg, editorial director, elementary language arts; Nick Savastio, creative group manager, advertising; Barbara Schneider, vice president, publishing services; Altienne Hahn, Louise McNutt and Richard Peterson.

Drew Hodges, Adam Levite and Naomi Mizusaki at Spot Design worked with good humor and enthusiasm to give Dick and Jane the design they deserve. Susan Jonas and Marilyn Nissenson provided valuable research on which the writing of this book is based, and George Rosato and Patricia Harrison were especially helpful consultants on education issues. James Keeline, The Prince and the Pauper, San Diego, shared information, materials and insights. David Thompson, WTVP-TV47 Peoria, producer/director of the television documentary *Whatever Happened to Dick and Jane?* and co-curator of a traveling exhibition of Dick and Jane watercolors, has been supportive and generous with sharing his original research. A special thanks to Bob Keeshan and Ruth Manecke. Thanks to Maurice Berger for encouragement and advice.

Other individuals to whom we are grateful for their help and encouragement include: Allison Anderson; Gary Kraut, Alphaville, New York City; Allan Chasanoff; George Darrow, Fun Antiques, New York City; Derek Nelson; David Newell; Nancy Hart, director, Clinton County Historical Society and Historical Museum, Frankfort, Ind.; Maria T. Olmedo; and Kathleen Woith, director of marketing and public affairs, Lakeview Museum of Arts and Sciences, Peoria, Ill. Thanks to Jocelyn Clapp, UPI/Bettmann, Inc.; Michael Shulman, Archive Photos; Christine Argyrakis, FPG International; Roberta Groves, H. Armstrong Roberts and Ron Mandelbaum, Photofest.

Picture Credits

A

A-bomb 59, 75
Advertising 12, 13, 14, 38, 57, 58, 82, 86, 104, 106
African-Americans 60, 64, 75, 93, 96, 101
Allyson, June 23
American Dream 1, 11-13, 44, 54-61, 64, 75, 93, 106
Appliances 57, 59, 63, 64
Armstrong, Jack 12
Automobiles 13, *56-57*, 57, 58, 81, 82, *82, 83*, 84-85, *84-85*, 102

B

B-29 12, *12*
Baby boomers 1, 14, 30, 38, 57, 81, 82, 86, 92-96
Backyards 58, 64, 66-67, *66-67*, 99
Bad Seed, The 24
Baldwin Readers 25
Barbie 38
Beatles 93, *93*
Berkeley demonstrations 92, *92*, 94
Black power movement 101
Brown v. *Board of Education of Topeka* 101
Buck, Pearl S., 46

C

Campbell, Eleanor 21, 31
Carrol, Diahann 101
Chatty Cathy 38, *38*
Children
  consumers 14, 20, 57
  discipline 10, 11, 64
  labor laws 10
  sophistication 86, 96
  working 10, 11, 12, 13
  World War II orphans 13, 42
Child Study Movement 10
Cities 10, 25, 51, 92, 101
Civil rights movement 93, *93*, 94, 101
Clark, Kenneth B. 101
Cleaver, Beaver 20, *20*
Cold war 59, 75, 92
Comic books 69, 86, *86*
Communism 58, 64, 75
Conformity 57-58, 59, 60, 75
Coogan, Jackie 12
Cosby, Bill 101
Crayolas 38
Crockett, Davy 38
Crosby, Bing 13
Cuba 92

D

Dennis the Menace 20, *21*
Depression, the Great 1, 11-13, 14, 17, 19, 36, 75
Dewey, John 11
Dick 16-20, *16-20*
Dick and Jane readers 1, 10, 14, 17, 20, 21, 25, 43, *43*, 56
  Big Books 43
  Cathedral editions 74, *74*
  competing series 81, *81*
  criticism 106
  design 21, 43
  development of characters 1, 21, 31
  health editions 74, *74*
  illustrations 21, 25, 26, 31, 88, 96
  influence 1, 21, 25, 43, 57, 72-73, 89, 93, 106
  interpretation of pictures in 43
  marketing 56, 89, *89*, 101, 106
  multiculturalism 96, 101, 106
  origins 21
  pre-primers 21, 25, 43, *43*
  primers 43, *43*, 106
  Seventh Day Adventist edition 74
  stereotypes 106

Teacher's Editions 43, 74, 78-79, *78-79*
  updating 43, 74, 96, 102-103, *102-103*, 106
  vocabulary 21, 32, 43, 70, 74, 88, 102, 106
  workbooks 43, *43*, 88
Ding Dong School 96
Dionne Quintuplets 12
Disneyland 38
Divorce 14, 93
Donna Reed Show 49
Drugs 46, 60, 95, 96
Duck and cover 59, *59*

E

Education 25
  compulsory 10
  elementary 12, 95
  expansion in 30, 92, 94, 101
  progressive movement 11
  strain under baby boom 30, 78, 92
Eisenhower, David 77
Eisenhower, Dwight D. 57, *57*, 64, 77, 82
Elson Readers 21, 25
Evers, Medgar 101

F

Family 1, 24, 25, 36, 41, 45, 48-49, *48-49*, 53, 59, 106
Family Circle 33, 38
Farms 10, 33, 38, 43, 50, 52-53, *52-53*, 64, 77, 85
Father 40-42, *40-41*
Father Knows Best 49
Flesch, Rudolf 106
Fortune 30
Franchises 82
Francis, Connie 92
Free Speech Movement 94
Freud, Sigmund 10
Friedan, Betty 46

G

Gallaudet, Thomas 25
Garland, Judy 12
Gay liberation 94
General Motors 82
GI Bill of Rights 14, 42, 64
Graham, Billy 59
Grandparents 50-51, *50-51*, 100
Gray, William S. 1, 21, *21*, 25, 43

H

Hall, G. Stanley 10
Hitler, Adolf 12
Home 14, 24, 57, 62-63, *62-63*, 64
Home front 13-14

I

Immigrants 10, 25

J

Jane 22-24, *22-24*
Johnson, Lyndon B. 93
Joplin, Janis 92

K

Kennedy, John F. 92, *92*
Kerner Commission 101
Khrushchev, Nikita 59, *59*, 64
King, Martin Luther, Jr. 93, 101, *101*
Kinsey, Alfred 59
Korean War 42, 57, 59

L

Ladies Home Journal 46
Lassie 20, *20*
Leave It to Beaver 20, *20*
Levittown 64, *64*
Levitt, William J. 64
Life 30, 46, 58, 86

Lindbergh, Charles A. 11, *11*
Little League 58
Little Orphan Annie 23
Lone Ranger 12
Look 58, 86
Love-ins 95, 96, *96-97*
Lucy van Pelt 24, *24*

M

Malcolm X 101
Mann, Horace 25
Mathers, Jerry 20, *20*
Maynard, Joyce 30
McCall's 46, 56
McCarthy, Joseph 58, 59, *59*
McCormack, Patty 24, *24*
McGuffey Readers 25
Media 12, 13, 58, 77, 88, 92, 93, 96, 104
Mike 96, *97*, 98-99, *98-99*, 102
Mobility 12, *56-57*, 57, 58, 82, *82*, 84-85, *84-85*, 92
Montgomery Ward 26
Moon landing 95, *95*
Mother 44-45, *44-45*
Motherhood 26, 44, 45
Motown 101
Movies 11, 12, 13, 20, 24, 46, 58, *58*, 69, 70, 77, 86, 88, 92
Mr. Potato Head 38, *38*
Mussolini, Benito 12

N

Nancy 24, *24*
National Geographic 86
North, Jay 20, *21*
Nuclear family 46, 49, 59, 93

O

Oral contraception 95, *95*
Ozzie and Harriet 49

P

Pam and Penny 96, *97*, 98-99, *98-99*, 102
Parent-Teacher Associations 30, 46
Parker, Fess 38
Peace Corps 92, 93
Peale, Norman Vincent 75
Pearl Harbor 12, 13, *13*
Phonics 21, 25, 43
Pilgrims 10
Polio 59, 77, *77*
Postwar WWII life
  affluence 14, 20, 30, 38, 46, 57, 61, *61*, 88, 92, 94
  consumers 14, 30, 56, 86
  housing 56, 57, *57*
  insecurity 59, 60, 75
  women in work force 46
Presley, Elvis 59
Puff 34, *34*

R

Radio 12, 13, 63
Reading
  content 25
  history 25
  importance to democracy 25
  literacy 25, 43, 104
  phonics 21, 25, 43, 79, 104
  readiness 43, 86
  technique 1, 20, 25
  theory 25, 78, 106
  whole word 21, 25, 43
Redbook 46
Religion 58, 59, 60, 72, 75, 82
Rettig, Tommy 20, *20*
Rogers, Ginger 23
Romper Room 96
Rooney, Mickey 12

S

Salk, Jonas 77
Sally 31-32, *31-32*
Science fiction 60, 86, 95
Scott Foresman 1, 21, 25, 43, 74, 78, 106
Scouting 46, 75, 77, 77
Sears Roebuck 26, *26*, 86
Segregation 59, 75, 96, 101
Selma march 93, *93*
Sesame Street 104, *104*
Sex 59, 95, 96
Sharp, Zerna 1, 21, *21*, 30, 31
Silly Putty 38, *38*
Smith, Kate 13
Soviet Union 59
Spock, Benjamin 56
Spot 32-32, *32-33*
Sputnik 60, 75
Suburbia 14, *15*, 20, 45, 46, 56-60, 59, 64, *64, 65*, 67, 75, 92, 101
Superman 13
Supreme Court 75

T

Teachers 21, 25, 30, 43, 51, *51*, 78, 88, 96, 101
Technology 56-60
Television 20, 30, 34, 38, 49, 58, 60, 63, 69, 75, 86, 88, *89*, 92, 96, 100, 101, 102, 104, *105*
  advertising on 30, 38, 58
  educational *87*, 104, *104*
  hours watched 86
  situation comedies 49, *49*, 101
  violence on 92, 93, 96
Temple, Shirley 11, *11*, 12, 23
Textbooks 11, 21, 43, 106
  early editions 21, 25
  illustrations 21, 25, 43
  moralism and patriotism 21, 25, 72
  multiculturalism 96, 106
  vocabulary 21
Tim 35, *35*
Toys 20, 36, 38, *38*, 102

V

Values 69, 70-72, *72-73*, 75
Vietnam War 92, 94, *94*, 95
View-Master 60, 86
Visual literacy 43, 79, 86, 104

W

Whole word method 21, 25, 43
Wilson, Charles E. 82
Woman's Day 46
Women's magazines 46
Women's movement 46, 94
Woodstock 94, *94-95*
World of Dick and Jane
  fashions 17, 23, 25
  fun 1, 17, 25, 36-37, *36-37*, 67, 102
  humor 19, 29, 32, 36, 48
  responsibility 17, 25, 31, 32
  stamps *12*
  trouble 18, 25, 35, 49, 76-77, *76-77*
  work 33, 38, 41, 44-45, 67, 69, *71*, 99, 102
  values 19, 24, 31, 41, 69, 70, 72-73, *72-73*
World's Fair, 1939 12
World War II 1, 12-14, *12, 13*, 17, 19, 38, 42, 46, 51, 75, 78, 95
  casualties and deaths 13
  children's part 12, 13, *13*, 19
  economic boom 13, 14, 20, 30
  entertainment 13
  fathers 13, 14, 42, *42*
  housing loans 14
  mobility 13
  savings 13, 46, 64
  shortages 13
  women in 46, 78

111

First published 1996
by Collins Publishers
10 East 53rd Street
New York, New York 10022

Produced by Lookout
1024 Avenue of the Americas
New York, New York 10018

HarperCollins Web Site: http://www.harpercollins.com

Library of Congress Cataloging-in Publication Data
Kismaric, Carole, 1942-
Growing up with Dick and Jane: learning and living the American dream/
Carole Kismaric, Marvin Heiferman: preface, Captain Kangaroo/Bob Keeshan.
p. cm.
A Lookout Book.
ISBN:0-06-076681-6
1. Readers (Primary)—History and criticism. 2. Children—Conduct of life—Study and teaching—United States—History.
3. Education (Primary)—United States—History—20th century. 4. Reading (Primary)—Social aspects—United States.
5. Textbooks—United States—History and criticism. 6. United States—Civilization—20th century. I. Heiferman, Marvin. II. Title.
PE1119.3.K57 1996
428.6'083—dc20   95-40246

Printed in Hong Kong
20 19 18 17 16 15 14